# Having It All?

## Choices for Today's Superwoman

### Professor Paula Nicolson

University of Sheffield

JOHN WILEY & SONS, LTD

This publication is designed to provide accurate and authoritative information in regard
to the subject matter covered. It is sold on the understanding that the Publisher is not
engaged in rendering professional services. If professional advice or other expert
assistance is required, the services of a competent professional should be sought.

*Other Wiley Editorial Offices*

John Wiley & Sons, Inc., 111 River Street, Hoboken, NJ 07030, USA

Jossey-Bass, 989 Market Street, San Francisco, CA 94103-1741, USA

WILEY-VCH Verlag GmbH, Boschstr. 12, D-69469 Weinheim, Germany

John Wiley & Sons Australia, Ltd, 33 Park Road, Milton, Queensland 4064, Australia

John Wiley & Sons (Asia) Pte, Ltd, 2 Clementi Loop #02-01, Jin Xing Distripark,
Singapore 129809

John Wiley & Sons Canada Ltd, 22 Worcester Road, Etobicoke, Ontario M9W 1L1,
Canada

**Library of Congress Cataloging-in-Publication Data**
A catalogue record for this book has been requested

**British Library Cataloguing in Publication Data**
A catalogue record for this book is available from the British Library

ISBN 0-470-84687-9

Project management by Originator, Gt Yarmouth, Norfolk (typeset in 11.5/13pt Imprint)
Printed and bound in Great Britain by Biddles Ltd, Guildford and King's Lynn
This book is printed on acid-free paper responsibly manufactured from sustainable
forestry, in which at least two trees are planted for each one used for paper production.

# Contents

# About the author

Paula Nicolson is Professor of Health Psychology at the School for Health and Related Research (ScHARR), University of Sheffield, UK. Her research interests are in women's reproductive health, including sexual behaviour and postnatal depression, and gender/power relations at work. She is author of several books, including *Postnatal Depression: Facing the Paradox of Loss, Happiness and Motherhood*, published by John Wiley & Sons in 2001 in the *Family Matters* series.

*To Malachi, with love*

# Acknowledgements

I would like to thank Viv Ward and her team at John Wiley & Sons for inspiration, support and patience. My family and friends were always at hand, in different ways, to entertain, look after and inspire me, as I wrote and tried to keep to my deadlines. I am grateful to you all.

# Introduction

*Who should read this book, and why?*

*A liberated woman is one who feels confident in herself, and is happy in what she is doing. She is a person who has a sense of self ... It all comes down to freedom of choice.*[1]

*Women are the labouring sex. From the time girls are very small they learn that work is what time is for. Comparison of women's work-load with men's is difficult because a good deal of women's effort is not even recognised as work. Time spent with the children is not classified as work, although the mother does not use this time to read the paper while the kids crawl between her legs, but to teach her child to speak, to advance its social skills, to answer its questions, to deal with its preoccupations, to prepare it for school activities.*[2]

Over the past 150 years or so women in Western societies have sought and found liberation in a number of ways.

We have achieved the vote, equal human rights and opportunities, the right to a career, choice as to whether to marry, have children, to be working mothers, to access economic and legal independence from men, sexual liberation and psychological freedom. These freedoms have been obtained at a price, and they are distributed unevenly among us.

The present generation of working women, have had opportunities that previous generations did not even dream about. We have successfully set up and run our own companies, entered and flourished in the professions, earned high salaries, entered public life and become 'captains' of industry and commerce. Not only that, most of us have entered long-term relationships with a partner, shared children, maintained an active social and cultural life and attended to our appearance, health, home and garden. In short, it has become possible for women to *have it all*, and many of us have strived and succeeded in achieving this goal. But while many women have become today's Superwomen, successful at home and at work, many of us are also giving up on what we have strived for so long – *having it all* has become the same as *doing it all*, and that has put a major strain on our emotional and physical resources. This has led to some high-profile rejections of public life, fame and career in favour of the family, which has fed into a 'backlash' – accusations that we are not fit for careers and high-profile occupations, but should return to the home, or take up less pressured occupations.

At the turn of the millennium, a survey conducted by the University of Bristol in the UK for the British Broadcasting Corporation (BBC) demonstrated that a third of working mothers chose to work part-time or give up work. One of their respondents said that she felt so guilt-ridden about both home and work, that she 'couldn't bear to carry on'.[3] In September 2001 a UK Government-backed research programme from the Policy Studies Institute suggested that:

> *Women who combine work with children are having a worse time now than a decade ago and are increasingly dissatisfied with the number of hours they are working.*
>
> *On average working mums are spending an additional two and a half hours a week at work compared to the early 1990s.*[4]

This article was followed by a comment from Shirley Conran, author of the original *Superwoman* in the 1980s, from which the term was coined to describe women who do it all, to have it all.[5] Conran claimed that children whose mothers work such long hours faced poor education, health and job prospects and that one in five children today face stress-related problems.

But what is the answer? It is clear that it is *not* leaving work. Most women work for psychological, economic and social reasons. We know that families with young children are among the poorest in Western societies. We also know, that even for affluent families, the years of parenthood are those when finances need to stretch further than at any other time in the family life cycle. More than that, a great number of women become frustrated, unhappy or even clinically depressed if they engage in full-time motherhood and forego career opportunities. Being at home with a depressed or unhappy parent is stressful for children and can reduce the child's ability to learn and meet its academic and social potentials.

The solutions to all these problems remain elusive. While children's fathers need to take on more responsibility for child care and domestic chores, it is clear that this is not happening to the extent that it is making a difference to the lives of women or children. We know that many women are talented beyond the mother/house-wife role and commerce, industry, the professions, governments and public offices desperately *need female talent*.

There are pressures that challenge the role and belief systems of today's Superwomen that is a backlash against women's increasing power and influence per se. There are growing numbers of articles and books that suggest women should 'return' to the home and hearth. For example, Danielle Crittenden's book, *What Our Mothers Didn't Tell Us: Why Happiness Eludes the Modern Woman*, suggests that women are unhappy because:

> *they are pretending to be the same as men with similar needs and desires (which) has only led many of us to find out, brutally, how different we really are. She believes that when it comes to negotiating the balance between love, family, friends and work, 'feminism has failed women'.*[6]

There is now an increasing public profile of women who have left the rat race – seen the light and returned to the home. On closer inspection this is seen to be inspired and promoted by pro-family, religious, conservative groups, but for Superwomen who are feeling the strain at home and at work, there are probably a great many occasions when they are tempted to give it all up in favour of 'their families'.

But this is not necessary – leaving work does not reduce the strain of life beyond perhaps short-term relief. Superwomen work because they need the stimulation and excitement of their chosen career – otherwise they wouldn't have got so far. Balance and peace of mind are not about giving up what you value in your life and where your skills are important – they can be achieved by different means.

This book, *Having it All? Choices for Today's Superwoman*, is aimed at those of us who have it all, or want to have it all, while maintaining our health and sanity. The aim is to show how we can manage our lives, succeed at what we are doing and reduce stress and anxiety – in short get pleasure from what we do rather than be on a 24-hour, 7-days-a-week, treadmill. The book demonstrates and identifies potential traps in the life of a Superwoman and shows how to avoid them *without having to give up on what you want and what you believe in.*

This book helps those who aspire (or might have aspired) to be Superwomen to make more *personal* choices – to choose their individual pathway to success, personal growth, change and self-confidence and to find ways to win in their own terms. To cope, emotionally and psychologically, with the challenging world of the 21st century where Western women have (at least legal) equality with men and where that equality frequently means increased responsibility, stress and pressure – at home and at work. The first lesson for Superwoman is to recognise that *we* heap these additional loads *on ourselves* just as often as others expect and demand super-natural responses. This book shows how we can *make choices that suit us as individuals*, and become more effective and emotionally able in the *ways we have chosen for ourselves*. Looking after ourselves, though, does not mean neglecting other people or our wider responsibilities as mothers, partners, employees, friends or colleagues. It means that we are able to be there for others when it is appropriate. Then we have the time, means and energy.

So what might we *lose* if we are to be more aware of our own needs? What will other people think of us? Will you turn into a mean, self-centred, uncaring and ultimately unlovable/unloved person? When you start to think of how to be yourself without aspiring to total perfection, *panic* sometimes sets in. There is a *psychological gap* in your sense of who you are. If I don't try to succeed in all parts of my life who am I? What is left?

The answer to this is always an individual one. Women have much in common but we are more than *just* women. We have a personal history, our own personality, a unique genetic make-up and other factors that make us who we are. Trying to become the perfect woman does not help us to become more attuned to our unique sense of self. It alienates us from who we really are.

By the time you have read this book you will know the *kinds of personal choices* that you yourself need to make to avoid aspiring to the Superwoman myth. You will be able to diagnose your potential for falling for the siren call of the Superwoman aspiration. You will be able to find your own ways to win, to play the game that enables you to be personally effective and secure in who you are rather than what other people want or expect you to be – or what *you think* other people expect of you!

What follows in this book is structured around two aspects of psychology. The first is about *personal psychology*. How we experience the internal pressures to have it all, to improve our life and to become today's Superwoman. Various theories from psychology and psychotherapy are employed to ensure that readers develop self-awareness.

The second aspect of the book is about the *psychological impact of the world around us* and how this can influence lives for better or for worse. The aim of the book is to enable readers to understand their *motivation to have it all* and then to *take back control* of their own lives through a deeper understanding of how, when and why we do what we do.

# Making choices

*Choices for today's Superwoman*

## Today's Superwoman

> *So much is expected of women today. It isn't enough just to do your best at home and on the job. We have to do it all. We're expected to be the perfect wife and mother, the impeccable house-keeper, the brilliant career woman ... all at once. We have housework, homework, gardening, cooking, family time and overtime to juggle. On top of that, we're still supposed to find time to work out and eat right. After all, we've got to do a little something for ourselves, right?*[1]

Superwoman has come under inspection. What does it mean to be a Superwoman? Is she really super? Does being Superwoman mean having to *do* it all or aim to *have it all*? Do the career and family prospects for women in the 21st century create a whole new set of obligations for us or do they genuinely give us choices? The

answers to these questions are the subject of this book.
What follows is intended to inform the reader and stimulate ideas about our lives as contemporary women. We
have the chance to *gain* education, career, family, good
health and social, artistic and other skills and benefits
which were not available to our mothers and grandmothers. However, along with these, come *obligations
and expectations for* ourselves. This means hard work
and abundant energy.

If we are not born having it all we feel obliged and
excited about trying to achieve it. In the process we
think we also have to *do it all*. This is stressful, tiring
and potentially unhealthy and unrewarding.

What does it mean to 'have it all'? We all know of other
women, and men for that matter, who seem to *have* everything – good looks, career success, a perfect relationship,
wonderful children, money, good taste, self-confidence
and a lifestyle that does justice to all of these things. But
how do they achieve these things? Are they worthy, more
so than we are? Were they born lucky, with a silver spoon
in their mouths? Do they have the alchemist's power to
turn base metal into gold? Or do we see them as cheats,
charlatans, dishonest and unfair players? Are their lives
based on privileges that are undeserved? How might *we*
have it all?

The answer to this question is complex and often in-
consistent. It doesn't make sense when we see others
getting things they don't appear to deserve. Nor is it
fair, that despite our best efforts we do not have the
things that some others seem to acquire with ease –
whether we are talking about possessions, relationships
or psychological attributes such as an assertive personality
or friendly disposition. When we think about having it
all we have to think about three areas of our life in
particular – *what we are like* as individuals, *what we can
do* about changing or developing what we have made of

our lives up to date and *how to cope* with feelings of inadequacy and envy that thoughts about others inspire.

In this book I explore the lives of women who appear to have it all, or who aspire to having it all or who have tried and given up, or perhaps more accurately, have taken a step back, looked at their lives and what is truly of value to them and modified their unrealistic, and frequently punishing, aspirations and behaviours. That is not to say that striving to achieve, seeking what is best for our loved ones and ourselves, is not of value. It is. To do things well and get the best from ourselves in most situations is an empowering, positive, life-enhancing and inspiring experience.

What is important is *how and why* we achieve what we do. We need to set realistic limits to our aspirations and goals and link the effort to the outcome. In other words we need to understand our potential and expend the amount and kind of effort that is required to achieve it. It is not healthy or in any sense beneficial to set out to accomplish things that others have attained *just because they have done it and we haven't*. To be truly successful we need to think *more* about ourselves, and of ourselves to gain a helpful and secure understanding of what is possible and find a means of peace in that knowledge. Beyond that lies the pathway to self-destruction via envy and a stressful lifestyle that finally leaves you exhausted and empty. But why should we have to discuss this at all? Surely it is common sense that we cannot and should not have it all? Our upbringing, the wider culture, religion, schools, universities, governments – all these institutions give out messages that suggest resources are limited. Even those with the greatest power and privilege in society don't all get what they want. How many of us can become President, Prime Minister, chief executives or top lawyers, doctors, journalists, artists and so on? By definition, very few of us.

However, for many women, the pressure has been on, particularly over the last 10 to 15 years. If there are opportunities to get into a high-status profession – better take it. If women can get to the top – better try. You are not truly realising your potential if you don't also have a partner and family. You are neglecting them if you don't give them quality time. You also need friends, and they need some of you too. What point is there in success if you lose your looks? The pressure is on and on. How does the average, talented, warm-hearted, potential Superwoman resist the pressures to have it all and remain sane and reasonably happy? How do you cope with the paradox that by *not* striving to have it all, by making sensible and realistic choices you might gain fulfilment? In what follows there is an attempt to solve this conundrum and help potential Superwomen to manage to be just that through gaining peace and emotional enrichment that comes with self-knowledge and confidence.

## Identifying the pressures: what we want, what we don't want

These days, an important part of a positive image is to appear physically fit and mentally alert, especially in the workplace. The working environment is increasingly competitive, and there is also a trend at present for one person to do the work of at least two people. So it is essential to look as though we can stand the strain and cope with the workload. Our personal lives are often just as demanding as we try to fit more and more into what may already be a hectic lifestyle.[2] Self-help manuals are encouraging:

*Making life easier should be the motto of every working mother – here you will find the practical help to do so. There's a no-need-to-think cookery section, including a stress-free guide to entertaining, plus a too-tired-to-think party planner for birthday bashes. You'll feel better if you can squeeze in time purely for yourself. There are plenty of ideas for recharging your batteries, with or without your partner, but definitely sans kids!*[3]

*Women are more determined than ever to get to the top. The problem seems to be that as they get closer, something stops them – the so-called glass ceiling. ... This book considers some of the main factors which contribute to this glass ceiling and suggests ways of breaking through.*[4]

Much has been written about women and how we can improve our lives. How we might be better mothers, move to the top in management, achieve the perfect relationship, be amazing cooks, juggle work and home, improve our body-image and self-esteem, learn to dress for success and heal our minds. It now seems possible for women to have it all – at home, at leisure and at work – provided we take the right advice and make the right decisions. The subject matter of advice-bearing books, magazines and television programmes is *how we, as women, might be better than we are*. The implication is that we are not *naturally* perfect women, but that *perfection can and ought to be achieved*. We owe it to ourselves, our loved ones, our colleagues and the rest of the world, to aspire to be *perfect*. We deserve to and can now *have it all*.

But where did these ideas come from? Why should we want to have it all? Why do we need to be perfect? What is 'perfection' anyway? Is the achievement of perfection a right or a responsibility? Do men experience the same pressures? Who determines the characteristics of the perfect woman? *What would happen to us if we let go of these aspirations?*

We all need to stop and think, to gain a balance in our lives. To do so brings with it personal effectiveness and peace of mind. For so long, the emancipation of women in Western societies has put pressure on us to achieve the (almost) unachievable: to be the perfect woman while winning in the world of men. We believe we have to succeed at work, because we have the opportunities, talents and abilities. We also believe, that because of those opportunities we have to prove ourselves even more so domestically. We are feminine and womanly, even while making it in the professional world that was formerly only open to men.

The pursuit of perfection in all things consumes endless energy and leaves us feeling like a leaking battery – never having the chance to recharge. This leads to mental and physical exhaustion. Experts call this the result of pursuing the *Superwoman syndrome*. Superwoman gained prominence in the late 20th century and, despite efforts to demolish her influence, she remains the icon of the 21st century Western woman. She makes the most of her opportunities and so seems to *have it all* – motherhood, love, fun, confidence, success and the admiration of others. Shirley Conran, who made a well-known attempt to demolish the myth, suggests that:

*I had noticed a growing anxiety and depression among ordinary women as the result of media propaganda about females who effortlessly organise a career (not a 'job'), home, husband, children and social life, while simultaneously retaining a 24-hour*

*perfect hairstyle and doing something esoteric, such
as learning Japanese in their spare time.*

*But I suspected that no-one could achieve every-
thing that the traditional woman was supposed to
do, let alone this demanding, exhausting, super-
achiever that threatened to depress our lives.*[5]

The conundrum we face is clear. Women have always
been expected (and expected themselves) to cope with a
great deal – to manage and support the lives of their
families, be physically and emotionally 'attractive' and
when necessary to earn money to supplement the main
income – but in the past we were supposed to have done
so quietly and leave the accolades, limelight and the glittering prizes to the men. Changes in sex-roles, techno-
logical advances in the home, educational opportunities
and economic changes have all led to increased opportunities and expectations for women. Women who *do* it all
(like the stereotype Conran describes above) also may
*have* it all. We are thus in a bind – there are these iconic
role models to live up to. Their lives seem to be glamorous, exciting and fulfilling. They also seem to achieve all
of these things with ease. The other side of the coin is that
there are not enough hours in the day to put in the work
towards perfection and to achieve it without some cost to
health. Thus self-help manuals show both how to achieve
and how to resist having to achieve as Superwomen. But
the myth will not disappear.


## Exposing the myth of Superwoman


Superwoman still needs to be exposed as a *myth*. So many
of us have tried to achieve the Superwoman distinction

but have inevitably failed. Superwoman is, by definition, *super-natural*. She cannot exist – and she should not exist because to live as Superwoman is to fail. She is the siren, luring women towards anxiety, stress and self-punishing. Choices can be made that are self-enhancing rather than self-admonishing. We need to heed our own needs, to be aware of our feelings and value ourselves for what we are and may choose to become in our own right. To do this, the first step is to understand the Superwoman myth for what it is and for what it might do for our self-esteem and need to achieve. The second step is to pay attention to who we really are and look after ourselves in that knowledge.

Consider the following essay question set for students of English literature:

> *'Elizabeth is one of the finest products of our civilisation – strong and intelligent, yet bewitching in a completely feminine way.' Discuss Jane Austen's portrayal of Elizabeth Bennet (in the novel* Pride and Prejudice) *in the light of this claim.*

Think also about the message underlying the headline ' "Superwoman" myth goes into retirement' in the *Houston Chronicle* in October 2001:

> *'I tried to be the perfect wife, mother, teacher, homemaker and lover', admitted a 52-year-old American academic. She went public to the media and her employer about her decision, after 3 decades of chasing the Superwoman myth, to have more 'balance' in her life.*

Superwoman Syndrome, in spite of this, seems to be alive and well, not only in our minds but also in the public consciousness. Various experts, psychotherapists, best friends, journalists and internet agony aunts, continue to offer advice to those who strive for power, love and feminine perfection and feel the strain. The paradox though is that the more consciously we recognise the Superwoman as an impossible achievement, the more we are exposed to images of the mythological in popular icons. In a recent magazine article[6] about Nicole Kidman, the movie star focused specifically on her struggles as a single parent following the break-up of her relationship with Tom Cruise. It was illustrated with model-style photographs of the 'talented Miss Kidman' and peppered by quotations from men colleagues:

> *I knew she would be a star when I first worked with her. She's extremely intelligent – and that is a rare thing in an actor, I'm sorry to say. You can actually have an intelligent discussion with Nicole about the purpose of a particular scene and what you want from it.*
>
>               (Geoffrey Burton, award-winning cinema-
>                     tographer and director who worked
>                          with Nicole on *Dead Calm*.)

and:

> *You meet a lot of beautiful people in this business but there's something almost luminous about her. I wish I had a clause in my contract that said Nicole Kidman had to be in all my movies.*
>
> (Joel Schumacher, director of *Batman Forever*.)

and:

> *She's also one of the funniest people I've ever met, as well as one of the most glamorous – but it's impossible to hate her.*
>
>               (Iain Glen, co-star in *The Blue Room*.)

The movie star herself though, in the piece about her life, comes across as modest, intelligent and self-effacing, attributing her strength in coping to the support of her women friends and the role model of her mother in particular. She says about her mother:

> *I adore her for her intelligence, her wit and what she gave up to help me and my sister. She could have been a doctor, but she chose not to be. She still worked through our childhood, but she was always there for us and gave us a great education and belief in our own power. When I was seventeen, she survived breast cancer, enduring chemotherapy and radiotherapy, and struggled with the notion of death. ... She's pragmatic and strong but still sweet.*

There is an endless cycle of pressure it seems – the movie-star icon has the perfect mother as her role model and protector. Superwoman is modest and owes all to another Superwoman. Kidman herself talks of her doubts, fears and weaknesses. The media image, though, uses those to strengthen her mythical status through the photographs and the quotations from those around her. We see the beauty, the strength and the modesty and thus the admitted weakness emerges as *strength*. How can we not at least try to be as good and as courageous as Nicole?

## Being true to yourself: making your own choices

What follows is aimed at all of us who have tried to achieve what (we think) other women have done – the dazzling careers, financial success, happy and fulfilling emotional lives, 'two plus' well-adjusted children, a strong and supportive intimate relationship, friends, a social life and popular acclaim as a strong, virtuous and feminine woman. And most of us have found ourselves wanting. Whether we gear up towards making even greater efforts at 'success' or make serious choices about our priorities, depends very much on how far we have absorbed the Superwoman myth into our hearts and how far we are prepared to face up to our limitations.

But why does the need to achieve in these ways touch upon our lives so strongly? Why should women strive for Superwoman status at all? How do we cope with the successes and the failures that occur every step of the way as we chase our aspirations?

The possible solutions to these dilemmas seem to be as angst-ridden as the questions themselves. For instance, should women as a group 'return' to full-time motherhood and concentrate on running the home? Should women make the choice between family and career? What is the 'balance' with which erstwhile Superwomen choose to supplement their lives? What price might be paid by womankind for the universal return of the Earth Mother? But wait ... even Earth Mother's 21st century incarnation – the 'domestic goddess' – is 'super'. She may not long for career success to the extent that her super predecessors did, but she does demonstrate excellence: in the nursery, in the kitchen and in maintaining her perfect appearance. Thus (we assume) she has a perfect relationship as well.

Most women who have travelled the route to Superwoman status reach a point where they have to cut their losses and minimise the 'collateral damage' that having it all brings about: the adverse effects on their family, friends and psychological and physical health. This seems unfair. Equality of opportunities and the legacy of feminism mean that talented women should have the right to seek the recognition and acclaim they deserve alongside their male counterparts. The problem is that men can choose to be successful at work and take on a minimal role at home and still be perceived as reasonable human beings; and, provided they don't inflict deliberate damage on the family, they are not criticised as 'bad' fathers.

Not so for women, of course. The 'good' mother and woman (and Superwoman has to be 'good') are only able to treat child care and career equally if the children thrive. Any threat to the children's welfare and she suffers – personal guilt and *public criticism*.

*The dilemmas surrounding the Superwoman Syndrome and how to cope with them are what follows.*

# The Superwoman Syndrome

*The heart of women's psychology?*

## Historical background

> *Superwoman has been rumbled. Juggling a career, a family and an active social life is quite literally a waste of time.*[1]
>
> *We have won the right to be terminally exhausted.*[2]

We may, as Western women at the start of the 21st century, have come full circle. From the exploited housewife of the 1950s, we have journeyed through the sexual liberation and feminism of the 1960s and 1970s, to the era of the successful female entrepreneur, manager or professional woman of the 1980s and 1990s. This has been at a price.

In the 21st century we have had to face up to what is missing from our busy lives during the overwhelming effort to achieve all – at any price. One woman's awakening went as follows:

*At four o'clock one morning, I sat in my darkened living room munching broken animal crackers. As I contemplated making a choice that would have profound consequences in my career, I was way too anxious to sleep. Inside my head I heard my father's voice telling me not to throw away my career. That was his value system. My husband's voice told me to stop anguishing and do something, anything, but to stop tearing myself apart. And from deep inside me I heard the voice of my mother telling me to lighten up. I didn't get to live my life, she said. So don't waste yours in worry. In this imaginary conversation I protested that I didn't know what was more important, work or home.*[3]

Elizabeth McKenna, the writer of these words, outlines the dilemma for today's Superwomen. We can be very successful. We can have it all – but the price is high. Superwoman status plays havoc with your physical and mental health. And yet, McKenna hears the parents who loved her egging her on. Don't spoil your career. Don't waste your life in worry. Get on and chase it all. Don't give up. This is the unfathomable contradiction at the heart of the Superwoman myth. Having it all comes along with a heavy penalty. Giving something up costs us dearly. Being a Superwoman is at the heart of the contemporary female personality – we have to be strong, we are responsible for others' welfare. If we are presented with opportunities – it seems sensible to take them. We have to achieve and we have to make sure that our loved ones thrive in our hands. But is there something particular about women that drives us so hard to succeed, to have it all and become a Superwoman?

# Women's minds and women's lives

Women, like men, are all unique human beings. We have an individual genetic make-up and a variety of lifetime experiences that all conspire to make us different from other women. Even twin sisters, however close, have different needs, aspirations and experiences. All women are different from each other. We are individuals. So is it helpful to talk about women and their psychology as if they *share something that distinguishes them as a group* from men?

Apart from *individual psychological and biological differences*, women, as biologically female members of the human species, do in fact have much in common. Genetically women have two X chromosomes (in contrast to men who have an X and a Y chromosome). Women's bodies share a sequence of physical development, which comes about because of these genes combined with the influence of female hormones. Women share a physical shape – they develop breasts, and have slim waists and fat around their hips. Women menstruate and thus have the physical capacity for conception, childbearing and breastfeeding. Many psychologists, from a variety of traditions, claim that women's *biological make-up alone* is enough to frame their lives in a particular way. For example, some psychologists such as the British evolutionary psychologist, Anne Campbell,[4] maintain that because women have such a great investment in each of their children,* women's minds have evolved to focus on

---

* This is because it takes a long time to conceive, give birth and raise a child and thus women are only able to have a small number of children in their lifetime. Men on the other hand can have a great many more, and their investment in each child is thus less.

what is necessary in order to nurture and raise those children. Women are thus biologically programmed through evolution, to be more nurturing and more able to take account of people's various needs in every situation than they are to be aggressive and competitive, pushing forward with their own agendas. This particular influence of evolution fits them emotionally and psychologically for certain roles (in the family, in management) rather than for others (as war leaders, or in the finance industry). Other psychologists, from the tradition of psychoanalysis based on the work of Freud, also see biology as an important determinant of women's minds. In this case, the gender-specific psychology comes about because of the infant's and adolescent's developmental relationship with their genitals and their unconscious recognition of the biological role and social symbolism of those genitals.

Further, and of equal importance, are the arguments that women's place in *all* societies has set us apart from men. Men tend to hold power – in the family, in the community, in societies and internationally. Watching television broadcasts of meetings that set global agendas for trade, warfare, the environment or tackling world poverty – it is rare to see more than a small handful of women and some of those are there to support the main players – the men. Women are socially oppressed and their biology is used as an excuse for that oppression.

Whatever theoretical position you come from, it is certain that women's lives (at least for a few significant years of their lives) revolve around the home. The extent to which their focus is on the home varies. Some women have babies and return to work a few weeks later. Others spend several years as full-time mothers. But, whatever the choice they make about the proportion of their time they spend outside the home, their sphere of responsibility *specifically includes the domestic arena*. Rhona and Robert Rapoport[5] in their study of dual-career families in the 1970s, showed quite clearly that aspiring and highly successful professional women, even when no children were involved, were responsible for the couples' domestic and social arrangements while their husbands focused primarily upon their work. Contemporary studies show little has changed.

This all has an impact on what women expect of themselves and of other women. It has an impact on what men expect of women and what the children we bring up see for their future. Women's lives as mothers shape much of what happens to them and to their children. Motherhood, largely invisible to the wider world, sits in stark contrast to international diplomacy or everyday professional life. We are constantly surrounded by images of politicians, lawyers, doctors, superstars. We do get images of women as mothers but they tend to be either of women who cannot cope, knee-deep in nappies and fraught from the demands of their various children, or Superwomen, for whom these chores and considerations are mere trifles. So women *do* have a common psychology based on their biology, or their life experience or their social status, or a combination of these. This influences our aspirations and achievements as well as our view of other women and of men. The importance of women's psychology is a major theme throughout this book because, without an understanding of our psychology, we can neither appreciate nor recognise the stresses, strains and achievements in our lives; nor can we gain the benefit that comes from that understanding, which is learning how to conquer them.

## Who is a Superwoman?

*The radiant Yulia Tymoshenko, the opposition leader in Ukraine, put glamour firmly on the agenda for women in the former Soviet Union when she revealed her beauty secrets in* Harpers & Queen *recently. Despite her busy life campaigning for the parliamentary elections, Ms. Tymoshenko found time to tell readers, rather improbably for one of the richest women in the country, that she relies on soap and boiled water to keep her skin blemish-free.*[6]

*Role models* are an important influence on our lives. They are individuals whom we admire and aspire to imitate. They include real people, such as our mother, older sister, favourite aunt, a teacher, a colleague or a friend, and they may be fictional characters or celebrities. We take account of role models throughout our growing up, but also in adulthood. How does an admired friend deal with her children, or a well-liked colleague with pro-motion opportunities? We don't have to know the role models personally to learn from them, nor do they have to be real. Fictional characters can be as inspirational as our friends.

But how does someone become our role model? We tend to choose role models who bear some relationship to what we know about ourselves already. If we have athletic or sporting aspirations, then we look for successful women in these fields to provide inspiration or encouragement. If we see a senior female colleague at work who shares some of our personality traits or values what we value, then we might adopt her as a model. We have done this from a very early age. It serves to modify and develop sophistication in our behaviour. Role models enable us to understand what society values in women's behaviour and thus each of us develops our behaviours, beliefs and aspirations in line with the characteristics of socially valued people.

Nicole Kidman, or at least the image we are provided

of Nicole Kidman, is someone who fits the bill. She is a potential role model for Superwoman who in turn modelled herself on her mother. However, Kidman said that her mother could have been a doctor but instead 'dedicated her intelligence and compassion to her family'. We see from this, that we don't simply copy our role models. We inject our own meaning into how we understand their lives and lead our lives accordingly. Individual role models might be a great influence on us, but only according to *how we interpret that influence as relevant to our own lives*.

Take the case of Sara. Sara, now a war correspondent for a television company, had a mother who had studied history and politics and then married a man who subsequently became a rich and successful businessman. Sara's mother never worked outside the home – either before or after taking her degree. She had three girls, live-in child care and an affluent lifestyle. But Sara gradually realised that her mother was totally dependent on her father – and not just for money. Her father made all the decisions in the household. When Sara was very young, she thought her mother had the power, because her nanny was answerable to her mother as were Sara and her sisters. Sara loved her mother and wanted to be like her. But this power she perceived that her mother had when she was small turned out to be a limited sphere of influence. Sara, who still admired her mother enormously, chose to study the same subjects at university, but wanted to do so, in order to live out the life she felt her mother might have had.

We don't all have close contact with potential role models we admire. We frequently rely on the media for our inspirations. Glossy magazines are full of examples of women similar to Kidman and we only need to read a few of the articles that describe their lives to realise what is required if we are to live up to their standards:

*She's one of the most successful women in British Music, but Sharleen Spiteri refuses to let fame go to her head. And she doesn't mince her words about people who do.*[7]

*Trudie Styler may be famous for being Sting's wife, but her achievements to date are pretty impressive film producer, successful charity fundraiser, documentary maker and now star of new film* Me without You. *Stuart Husband catches up with her during a break in her hectic schedule.*[8]

These headline introductions to celebrity interviews, both of which were in the same issue of the magazine *Marie Claire* (aimed at the 30-something, intelligent but stylish woman reader), use the prefix 'super' to describe these women whose personalities embrace professional brilliance which leads them to success, modesty, glamorous marriages, altruism, energy and a clear sense of who *they* are, with an apparent lack of patience with lesser mortals. Their workload is enormous, but they take it in their stride. Furthermore, as with Nicole Kidman, they are each *shown* to be beautiful through the photographs that accompany the articles.

There is a convergence in all the descriptions of the contemporary Superwoman that imply that personal qualities, efforts and achievement inevitably result in a lifestyle that has it all.

There are variations on the theme, of course. For instance, while a Superwoman might be in show business as an actress or singer, equally she could be a successful lawyer, academic and member of the British House of Lords, as in the case of Helena Kennedy. Kennedy's Superwoman status is enhanced by her accounts of an impoverished working-class childhood in Glasgow – she came a very long way to achieve her outstanding success.

Superwoman could also be in business, an entrepreneur like Anita Roddick, founder of the *Body Shop* and spokeswoman on ecological and humanitarian issues.

The image and behaviours of Superwoman have changed over the decades. In the middle of the last century, Superwoman was often the power behind the throne  taking care of the home and the children and providing support and motivation to the man who 'provides' for her. Queen Elizabeth, the Queen Mother, was the supreme example of this. She supported her husband, King George VI, holding his hand when he delivered his speeches. She was revered as a wife, mother, grandmother and great-grandmother. The British people favoured her for these characteristics and for her acknowledged sense of fun *in that context*.

A woman with a more independent profile was frequently pitied because either she didn't have a man, or didn't manage to have one that was good enough. She was seen to be frustrated, unhappy or unfeminine. Thus women who made it in their own right, like Janis Joplin, ended up as ultimate losers.

As the 20th century wore on, Superwoman had a career of her own, but it supported or complemented rather than challenged her man's. The archetypal executive or politician's wife exemplifies this. Jackie Kennedy in the USA or Norma Major or Mary Wilson[9] in the UK were, in their different ways, the powers behind the throne. These particular kinds of Superwoman were renowned for their loyalty and putting their efforts into their families rather than their personal career advancement. But they also had independence in their elegance, beauty or appreciation of the arts, or in their writing poetry or prose. Women like this are still with us in abundance, but they are no longer contemporary icons or role models for the aspirant Superwoman. Presidents and prime ministers still have wives who become

well-known figures such as Hillary Clinton and Cherie
Blair. But they are also well-known as lawyers and political players *in their own right*. However, they still share the
dilemmas and suffer the brickbats of their predecessors. It
is their responses that are different – but those are stories
for later.

So who is Superwoman now? She is, of course, you
and everyone else with enough concern to be reading this
book. She is the woman who worries about how she can
succeed, care and cope with her responsibilities that
appear to grow the more she achieves. She is also concerned to look the part: be fit, beautiful, popular and
generous. She wants to be confident and think well of
herself without being conceited, and she does not want
to suffer torments of envy if she sees others achieving or
having what she herself longs for. Superwoman therefore
is the impossible dream. To go there wholeheartedly and
unprepared, is to court trouble, pain and anguish. Greater
understanding of the syndrome, and of the impossibility
of having it all, prevents disaster. Making choices, about
how to maximise your own potential and give and get
pleasure from life, leads to positive mental health. We
all need to gain a balance between the thwarted lives of
previous generations of women and the burnt-out state of
many of today's Superwomen. In order to make choices in
an informed way it is important to consider the history of
contemporary women.

## The history of today's Superwoman

*It was not until feminists of my own generation
began to assert with apparent seriousness that feminism had gone too far that the fire flared up in my*

> *belly. When the lifestyle feminists chimed in that feminism had gone just far enough in giving them the right to 'have it all', i.e. money, sex and fashion, it would have been inexcusable to remain silent.*[10]

There appears to a wide gulf between the image of the 'feminist' and that of Superwoman. Feminists are popularly (although not accurately) portrayed as aggressive and physically unattractive, and angry because, according to popular images, they have failed to gain what we are all supposed to want – a man. Although this is a crass summary of media images of 'the feminist', it is near enough the truth – so much so that many women currently under 35 would avoid the label at all costs. The generations who grew up in the 1950s and 1960s, as Germaine Greer (academic, author, literary critic, broadcaster and journalist) bemoans, are also not identifying themselves as feminists. At best some concede to be 'post-feminist'. The battle of the sexes, for liberation, has been won – they believe. They see their achievements in academia, business or the professions as *individual* achievements. Collective actions and critiques of society and gender or power issues are passé. We reap the rewards according to our own efforts – or at least that is how it might appear. But, like Greer, I believe that such an analysis is wide of the mark. Superwomen only exist because of the impact of feminism on women's lives.

## 'Superwoman Quits!!!' – reasoned withdrawal or backlash politics?

Women are only seen in their own right as achievers because of the increased belief in women's right to have equal access, with men, to power and social resources. But there is a growing, and increasingly visible backlash against women and their public success. For example:

*Superwoman Quits!!!*

*Let everyone know why you don't have to be Superwoman any more! Have some great fun proclaiming that ... SUPERWOMAN QUITS!*

*To become OWEG![11]*

This slogan comes from a religious-based web site which encourages women to give up the fight to have it all. The argument they offer is that there are other and better things that women can do in life than continue to strive for the glittering prizes that career and family life together might bring them. The assumption underlying this backlash is that the challenges to Superwoman are equivalent to challenges to feminism. The two are not necessarily related. Having it all does not mean the desire for women's emancipation. Equality and autonomy come at a high price. So many give up. Many are forced out through ill-health, or pressures connected with relationships with partners and children.

What is the answer? Why is it such a problem for accomplished and talented women to gain the kind of acclaim, rewards and status that equally (or less-) accomplished and talented men seem to accrue and enjoy with relative ease? While coming under the Superwoman category herself in many ways, Germaine Greer is above all a feminist. As such she has variously championed the needs of women to have economic and social equality with men as well as to be without men sexually and emotionally. She has made a strong case for women to choose to make their motherhood role a priority and to see it as an achievement.

She has declared that women don't have to make
themselves[12] available and attractive to men. Women
should be their *own people* – whatever that takes.

And that in a nutshell is the conundrum we face. As
women we are all different and have different backgrounds, tastes, lifestyles, resources and experiences. As
women though, we are different from men and throughout history that difference, rooted in biology, has been
exploited in such a way as to disadvantage women.
Women *as a group*, in almost all societies – advanced industrial, capitalist or rural, simple communities – have
been subordinated to men, *as a group*. That is, the
things that women do, whatever they are, are less valued
than the things men do. What each sex does, and the roles
they take, may vary from society to society or community
to community. But the power pattern is the same.

The Superwoman seems at first to be different. She
has power, status acclaim and all the other attributes of
influence. She is superior to many others, including many
men. However, what we see when we look closely is that
men have had a hand in Superwoman's creation – whether
it be a father, mentor, husband or lover. Men also have a
hand in her demise. When male favour and influence are
withdrawn the pressure is on – sink or swim – and the
latter is hard to achieve.

Jennifer, not her real name, was an ardent anti-
feminist, and greatly opposed to what she saw to be
'positive discrimination' in her chosen career in the
medical profession. At the age of 45 she became medical
director of a teaching hospital, which was no surprise as
she had always been both bright and ambitious. Jennifer
had worked hard at school and passed her exams with the
best possible grades. She decided to become a doctor, like
her father, and her achievements at medical school
mirrored her earlier ones at school. Her mother was a
kind, loving woman; but Jennifer has little more to say

about her than that. Her memories of childhood revolved around her relationship with her father who took her regularly to work with him from the time she was quite young. He showed her wonderful colour photographs from his medical books depicting various parts of the human anatomy. He would also promise financial rewards for passing examinations at school with a bonus for coming top of the class. The more she succeeded the more attention he paid her and when she went to study medicine at his old university, he let some influential friends know she was there. She immediately felt at home, special and keen to succeed. Her career was a glittering success.

However, she had a disastrous series of relationships with men, none of whom could match up to her father. Conversely several of her lovers accused her of not being 'feminine' because of the priority she gave to work. She married for a short time and had two children, neither of whom seemed particularly motivated academically, and she had great difficulty deciding how to handle her relationship with them. Jennifer became very upset when it was clear that they preferred to be with their father than with her.

Jennifer had lost all touch with women – she had no networks, advice or support that many women rely on to help them sustain and make decisions about relationships – at home and at work. When her private life began to get on top of her and there were difficulties in managing staff at work, she had no-one to talk to. She was a 'token' woman. When she was performing well, senior men claimed credit for getting her to the top. When things started to go badly wrong – and there was a scandal in the paediatric unit – they pulled the rug from under her and she had to leave and take a less prestigious job. Senior colleagues spoke out in meetings in ways that gave the impression that she should have had a better grasp of what had been happening. Not only did she realise she was not being supported, but she began to recognise that some of her trusted colleagues had kept things from her – she wasn't and never could be one of the boys.

## The heart and mind of Superwoman

Is the Superwoman phenomenon a product of a particular age or political era? Or does the archetype of Superwoman lurk within the hearts and minds of all women? Are we all ambivalent about the image? We seek to achieve perfection but fear success and thus denounce Superwoman for having too much: a feminist triumph too far. Perhaps women are their own worst enemies?

Sigmund Freud is attributed with the gesture of throwing up his hands during an address to his learned colleagues in exasperation saying 'what *do* women want'? The question has been famously debated in many public and private circles ever since – apparently with little success. It is rare though to ask a similar question about men. So what is so exasperating about what women might want? Why should women's demands and requirements be seen as separate from those of human kind as a whole – is there something specific or confused about women's desires? What is it that appears to define us in this way as a group with conflicting wishes, ambitions and needs?

## What women want

The 'problem' of what women want is one that has challenged *men* deeply over the ages. It is only recently that

women have had so many choices – mainly because of
economic improvements in our lives. In previous eras
women were forced to gain or maintain their status
through marriage or through being beautiful enough to
attract powerful lovers. Women therefore needed to
know how to manipulate a man into marriage or to bed
and to keep them interested. Men themselves were rarely
ahead on the *emotional* game. However, as they continued
to enjoy their social, economic and political advantages
they were able to ensure that they had a woman there to
support them when required. Men rely on women for sex,
emotional support, companionship, running their domestic lives and caring for their children. In fact sociological
evidence makes it clear that men who are unmarried,
widowed or divorced are far less likely to be in good
health than are married or cohabiting men. Conversely,
women on their own tend to be as healthy if not healthier
than their married counterparts. Why should this be?

Emotions are important. Relationships are important.
And women are better than men at both. What is clear is
that men, many of whom find this state of affairs both
perplexing and intriguing, buy into a misogyny which
gets acted out in many ways, one of which is to portray
women as confused and confusing.

Women authors, journalists, psychologists and social
scientists in particular have always shown a talent for
writing about the conundrums that surround women's
lives – love, money, marriage, motherhood, social status
and ways of surviving in class-ridden societies where male
power is paramount. Women have studied women.
Women do know what they want – they also know that
they have to find circuitous routes around various
systems. How do you survive/reach the top in your work
organisation? How do you cope with the competing
demands of your partner and children? How do you
manage work, the role of housewife and mother and

remain able to lavish some of your precious resources on yourself?

What happens in most societies though is that it is not *women* who identify and act upon what they want. What women 'want' is defined and controlled by *men in power*. This includes men who make the rules and the men in the lives of women at work and at home who ensure that those rules are adhered to. As one man put it:

> *I hope to show that misogyny is universal, and that it has profound effects on men's and women's capacity for creative and healthy living. The universality of misogyny consists in the fact that it is not only a facet of the male character but also an aspect – albeit a less debilitating one – of the female character.*[13]

## Controlling women's bodies and minds

While men argued that women were a 'puzzle', feminist writers were able to explain the underlying social and psychological structures in the relationships between men and women. Men ran societies and so needed to control women. One of the most influential ways that they achieve this is through the control of health. Women's health care throughout psychiatry, obstetrics and gynaecology has always been, and remains, dominated by men. Men thus pronounce on menstruation, menopause, fertility, childbirth, sanity and women's sexuality from their unchallenged viewpoint. The history of women in Western society is characterised by the efforts of male experts to make us appear weak, dependent, incompetent or sick. Women are frequently portrayed as 'mad' and unable to cope with the everyday problems of living when in fact they are triumphing over enormous odds. They are coping with domestic violence, motherhood, poverty and unhappiness.

Jane Ussher, a feminist psychologist and writer, suggests that what appears to be the *care* of women's mental and physical health represents a deeply ingrained misogyny, or hatred of women. She traces the modern origins of this from early psychiatry and gynaecology to contemporary mental health debates. However, what is most poignant in her book is the way individual women have coped with their lives, including her own mother:

*When I was an adolescent my mother was mad. Because it was the 1970s, she was deemed to be afflicted by her 'nerves'. Had it been 100 years ago, she would probably have been called 'hysterical' or 'neurasthenic'. Today it might be 'postnatal depression'. Her particular madness manifested itself in what was termed depression. Her unhappiness, pain and fear resulted in withdrawal, apathy, tiredness and a sense of worthlessness. Sometimes she cried. Sometimes she was angry. Being a 'good mother', a well-trained woman, as most of us are, she turned her anger in on herself, rather than outward on her four children, all under twelve years old. She didn't eat a lot. She 'let herself go' by eschewing nice frocks and neatly curled hair. Her outward anger was less evident: no doubt we missed a lot, intent on pretending that everything was normal at home and that we were a happy family.*[14]

Similar events and histories are discussed by Elaine Showalter describing what she calls the 'female malady'. She traces the history of women's 'madness', concluding that the only possible future for women is in a feminist understanding and approach to therapy where women's lives and women's standpoint are taken more seriously than male-dominated values and belief systems. It is

> ... *the feminist therapy movement* ... *[that is]* ... *essential to the future understanding of women, madness, and culture, and to the development of psychiatric theory and practice that, by empowering women, offers a real possibility of change.*
> ... *Until women break them for themselves, the chains that make madness a female malady* ... *will simply forge themselves anew.*[15]

It seems that madness is far from the character and achievements of the Superwoman. But look again! The journey from woman to Superwoman is paved with traps. High achievers have emerged from backgrounds where they are frequently well aware of the dangers that confront them. Sometimes, like Jane Ussher, they recognise that what happened to their own mothers is not very far removed from what might have been their own fate, were it not for the influence of feminism and the support and recognition of other women. Sometimes we get where we are going because of the support of a father, lover or husband. But without feminism we would have to expend much energy in reassuring these men that there was no threat to them or ourselves. Feminist efforts have made women and their lives visible. Not only have feminists challenged the value systems that identify women's distress as madness or weakness, *they have made us all visible.* We are fully functioning human beings. Our lives count.

Motherhood and what it means has now been described
and the skills and their value are now seen by all.

The lack of equal opportunities in the workplace is of
concern to Western governments. Women's welfare and
human rights are also of concern across the international
community. The health care, welfare and education of
women throughout Africa are acknowledged to be vital
if that continent is to survive the scourges of AIDs,
famine and warfare. Women's rights have been a major
item on the agenda in the reconstruction of Afghanistan.
There remains a long way to go in all these contexts.
However, women are now seen as significant in *all*
human societies for their mothering roles and for other
contributions at work and in the community. So how did
we get from feminism to Superwoman? What have been
the obstacles that she has had to overcome so far?

## Superwoman rising from the ashes

Women are weak, sensitive, unassertive, emotional, security-
oriented, tactful, gentle, interested in pleasing others,
concerned with their personal appearance, intuitive and
illogical. Women are not good at rational thought, objec-
tivity or being assertive. They are not at ease with success
because they are not competitive, confident, ambitious,
worldly, dominant or independent. Those characteristics
only apply to men. *At least that is what Sandra Bem*[16] *has
shown we have been led to believe*. Women want to be
feminine because that is an essential characteristic of
being a woman. But the paradox is that society devalues
those qualities, listed above, that are associated with femininity. But there have been times in our history when it
has been clear that this view of femininity and women's

personalities has been shown to be untrue. A well-documented and highly significant example was the way women were treated during and after the Second World War.

Women in Europe and North America at that period in history proved they could cope with running the home front. Women were involved in industry, commerce, service industries and the professions as well as domestic life. Women were also engaged in war work – organising communities as part of civil defence and ensuring people were sheltered from bombing raids and that no suspicious strangers infiltrated the community. Women made up most of the land army that provided agricultural labour so the population could be fed. Women were essential in the labour market and, without women's efforts, the military achievements of men would have failed. On both sides of the Atlantic, cinemas, newspapers and the radio all made appeals for women to take up employment to help in the war effort. Crèches and nursery places were made available for those who might otherwise be prevented from taking up employment by the demands of child care.

Women, it seemed, had come of age. The famous portrayal of the role of wartime women in the United States in the film *Rosie the Riveter* came to represent the energy and power that the autonomy and responsibility of work outside the home had given to women's lives. But of course, with the demobilisation of the armed forces after the war, women were returned to the hearth and home. The victorious allied governments were clear that *men* needed jobs. For the demobilisation to be successful women had to leave their work outside the home and become mothers and housewives again. And this is exactly what happened!

While many women, particularly those from the working class, wanted to continue to work outside the home for economic reasons, the government propaganda machines and the withdrawal of child care facilities drove them back. A combination of force (through drastically reducing nursery places) and propaganda (through making people believe that their children would suffer emotionally if they were separated from their mothers) had its effect. As Denise Riley[17] writes:

> *There was little to meet the practical needs of working mothers, although women with children did indeed gradually go out to unskilled and semi-skilled light industrial work more and more. ... Far from war work serving to revolutionise women's employment on any serious level, it was itself characterised as an exceptional and valiant effort, from which women could thankfully sink away in peace-time.*

Thus there had been an effective backlash even in the pre-feminist era. But as the decades passed, women once again found themselves in demand. However, as we made a success of our careers, subtle forces reappeared to encourage us back to the home.

## Conclusions

Never have women had so many opportunities to try out their abilities and develop themselves as fully functioning, intelligent, independent and dynamic human beings. Nineteenth-century beliefs about us − that we are passive, dependent, less intelligent, emotional, unassertive and over-concerned with our appearance compared to men – have given way to a more powerful and virtuous image. Women are *not* the same as men. But women are able to employ some of men's more desirable qualities, such as rationality, decisiveness and strength, while substituting some of the less pleasant characteristics of masculinity such as aggressiveness, lack of emotion, dominance and competitiveness with cooperative behaviours, nurturance and being aware of others feelings.

We all want to make the most of our potential. Unlike men, we can have babies. Like men, we can have successful careers. Many of us want to have it all, and why not? But unless we understand the rules for *psychological survival* we will suffer emotionally and physically. We will become anxious and stressed through having called on our resources time and again to exert superhuman qualities.

# Psychological survival and managing your 'self'

*The innocent self-acceptance with which we arrived at birth was a self-acceptance without an awareness of self. Our self was something which we had to construct.*[1]

Our sense of *self* is very important. On the surface – we all understand what 'self' is. My 'self' is 'me'. It is who I am and what I am like. In there somewhere also is our sense of our *future self* – the person who may be the powerful and successful woman who copes with and balances her life. It is our 'self' that we compare to the images of Superwoman. Our self is not static. We continue to change and construct our self over the course of our lives. That motivation for change comes from *somewhere inside us* and in order to be at ease with our self and to achieve balance and fulfilment we also need to understand that motivation.

The idea of self is very complex. This complexity is mirrored through the variety of the terms used to talk about the self. They include words such as soul, ego, identity, spirit, will, essence, personality, character, nature, integrity, make-up and individuality. The word 'self' is also added on to other words to describe a specific purpose of the self such as self-esteem, self-image, self-confidence, self-awareness, self-actualisation and so on. The self has several features that can be under our control and/or influenced by the environment. For some of us, self has a spiritual dimension. For others it is firmly rooted in biology or past experience. In whatever way we choose to understand the *idea* of self, *psychologically* we all have some experience of selfhood. There are a number of theories about the self, from social theories that personality is a product of the environment, to theories that personality is inherited and thus only minimally influenced by the social context.

## The psychodynamic approach

Psychodynamic theory is based upon the ideas of Freud who claims that we all have an unconscious as well as a conscious self. The human self, or psyche, is complex, contradictory and dynamic, and we feel, understand and respond to the world and others in relation to how we have coped in the past and how aware we our of our unconscious drives and needs. There are some aspects of our self that we inherit, some that are influenced by the outside world and others that rely *on the sense that we ourselves make of them.*

We may have been born beautiful and intelligent and had a good upbringing and education – but if we never stop to think of the impact we make on the world around us then we don't fulfil our potential. However, if we never stop to consider the impact of the world upon us – then we have lost a great deal more. We are unlikely to gain *peace* with *being ourselves.*

The work of psychoanalyst Erik Erikson focuses on the relationship of identity and the ability to cope with growing up and growing older in the context of the social world. He believed that over the life course an individual goes through a series of distinct developmental stages with a specific emotional task to accomplish at each stage. The stages are partly defined by cultural expectations, partly by biological stage and partly by the psychological context in which the child is growing. He also believed that any development task that is not successfully completed, leaves a residue that interferes with later tasks.

Although he based his theory on the eight ages of 'man'* it is not too difficult to see how Erikson's psychosocial stages of ego development relate usefully to Superwoman, particularly from adolescence onwards.

## The eight ages of Superwoman

The first year of life involves the infant in interacting with her caretaker, and it is the quality of that care that will give or deny the infant a sense of predictability or *trust* in the world. If the child's major experience leads to a sense of *trust* then the child is likely to go on to make successful relationships and have a positive sense of self. The second stage, of *autonomy* versus *shame and doubt*, takes place when the child has developed basic skills of communication and physical dexterity and mobility. At this stage she

---

* Although he meant mankind, his ideas have been criticised for overemphasizing men's life concerns.

| Age | Stage description | Emotional tasks |
|-----|-------------------|-----------------|
| 0–1 | Basic trust versus mistrust | Will the infant trust her caretaker? |
| 2–3/4 | Autonomy versus shame and doubt | Mastery of walking and other tasks – will she cope? |
| 4–5 | Initiative versus guilt | Will the child's new skills lead to too many mistakes? |
| 6–12 | Industry versus inferiority | Will the child be able to deal with intellectual tasks at school? |
| 13–18 | Identity versus role confusion | Adolescence – who am I? |
| 19–25 | Intimacy versus isolation | Can I be successful in relationships? |
| 26–40 | Generativity versus stagnation | Can I be creative? |
| 41+ | Ego integrity versus despair | Does my life make sense? |

**Figure 1**    The eight ages of Superwoman (adapted from Erik Erikson's psychosocial stages).

has gained some control over her bladder and bowels. If she makes too many mistakes in the learning process then she will increasingly develop a sense of shame rather than a sense of accomplishment. Once again the quality of the care she received will make a difference for better or ill.

*Initiative* versus *guilt* refers to the crisis around the child's ability to plan and take the initiative for some of her actions. She may also be interacting with other children during this stage. Again there is scope for a great many mistakes, and if the child is not supported by her caretakers she may experience too much of a sense of guilt about her failures.

Around the time of starting school, the emotional crisis is about *industry* versus *inferiority*. For the first

time the child is put into competition with several other
formerly unknown children. She is faced with the need for
approval from strangers, and that is achieved via the
quality of her work at school rather than her other personal qualities. If she doesn't do well, she risks feeling
inferior to her peers. The crisis for the adolescent is to
resolve the battle between developing a sense of *identity*
versus *role confusion*. There are so many opportunities and
obligations that a teenager might be faced with, including
those that surround sexual identity and the development
of relationships. Successful resolution of this crisis is the
development of an integrated sense of identity.

In young adulthood, during the crisis period of *intimacy* versus *isolation*, the task for the young woman is to
manage to develop close relationships without losing her
own identity.

The middle period of life,* *generativity* versus *stagnation*, involves creativity and development of self and one's
talents. The generativity might involve career, hobbies or
parenthood – and in the case of Superwoman it represents
generativity on a least two of those fronts. It is particularly
important to note that the opposite pole of generativity,
i.e. stagnation, is anathema to Superwoman.

*Ego integration* versus *despair*, the final stage, comprises the sum of life's parts. Did she manage to make
sense of her life, achieve what she sought in the way that
she wanted? If there are too many regrets, too many
unresolved issues from earlier in life, then a sense of hope-
lessness may set in for the last stage of life.

---

* Erikson's view that mid-life ends at 40 has been seriously disputed;
it is particularly uncharacteristic of women's experience because
many don't return to their career tracks until they are around their
early forties because of child care responsibilities.

## Presenting your self

The self is complicated. It continues to develop across the lifetime of an individual, and at each stage of life we pass through at each developmental crisis we confront, we fail to resolve some emotional issues. What we succeed in understanding and what we fail to see are all present in our selves, and elements of our self are presented in our dealings with others.

Negotiating contracts, doing battle in legal court-rooms, facing sick patients and their relatives or students in a seminar all involve us in presenting our professional self and, as far as possible, we have an idea of how we want and expect to be seen in those situations. When we are at home we are not the same as we are when we are at work or play. We don't want our children or partners to see us in the same ways that our clients see us. We want our children to know who we are and that we care for them, however they behave. That is not how we want our subordinates at work to see us. We manage our self-presentation quite consciously, although it does become second nature in familiar situations. However, when we are confronted with new circumstances and unfamiliar people and tasks to perform, it sometimes takes a while to identify what aspects of our self are most relevant and how we want to present our self in that context.

While we can become adept at negotiating self-presentation, there are also large components of our self that our clients and colleagues might identify of which we have little or no awareness.

*Margaret, a philosophy lecturer, was a strong fem-inist and taught classes on gender and thought. She was passionately committed to her research and teaching and particularly keen to encourage her students to work in the same area. Mostly it was the female students who did their chosen study options with her as it is usually women who are interested in gender. Margaret was always welcoming and enthusiastic, but was very distressed one day to find that her colleagues considered her to be a 'man-hater'. The idea was absurd to her. But to others around her, her encouragement of women students to study the topic of gender meant just that.*

*Why was Margaret, an academic of high intelligence, so unaware of the way that her enthusiasms came across to others?*

*Cindy was in love with a married colleague with whom she was having a sexual relationship. The colleague and his partner were friends of Cindy's family and most weekends they spent time together. Neither Cindy's nor her lover's partner or their children know of their involvement. Cindy's partner had been with her for 15 years and knew her well – but he didn't know about her other lover. She had been able to present herself as the loving faithful partner even though she was having an affair with someone else.*

*Eva wanted to present herself as gentle and compliant as she believed this was the most effective way of managing herself at work in a highly competitive sales team. She worked hard, with quite a good deal of success but did not want to be seen as too successful as she was aware of the kind of subterfuge that her colleagues might employ against her. However, she made some of her anger and anxiety clear in the language she used and the way she spoke to people – even though her words*

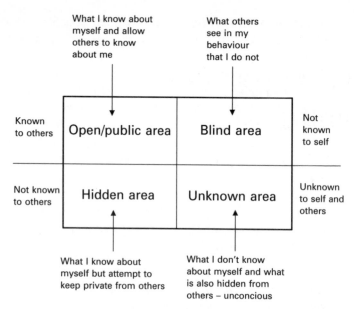

**Figure 2**　The Johari window.

*were presented in gentle tones. You didn't have to know her too well to realise that she was as competitive and hard-hitting as the others in her team.*

Margaret was surprised that others saw her in a way she believed was unrepresentative of how she really was. Cindy was good at hiding her feelings and behaviours from others. Eva was unaware of the feelings she had and also that they were available for others to see. In order to understand and handle ourselves better we all need to gain more understanding of the way others might see us.

The '*Johari window*' used by management consultants and psychotherapists is a simple device of self-knowledge and self-enhancement. This uncomplicated diagrammatic representation of the 'self' enables us to gain a sense of how we interact with other people and think about what other people might see when they interact with us. Developing our understanding of how we are in the world rather than just how we think and feel, enables us to gain greater self-knowledge, self-management, empowerment and empathy with others. In other words, the more we understand about our self, and the more we understand about the impact we make on others, the more likely we are to look after ourselves and those around us in a positive way.

Richard Kwiatowski and Dave Hogan[2] suggest that one way of gaining important insight into yourself and how others might see you is through thinking about how your profile changes in different teams or groups, and to consider why this might be the case. Thus for example what are the differences between the four areas represented by the Johari window at home, or at work, with friends? Friends (or at least the best and oldest) often know things about you that are in the open/public area that your partner may not know. You may have been told by friends, your partner or colleagues, about your blind area – do they all perceive similar things about you? What do you believe that others think are your blind areas? Again you might gain insight into the lives of colleagues and family if you try to think about their Johari windows. What blind areas do your colleagues have? What things are they keeping hidden? There are several theories about how we come to have a sense of who we are. Mostly they rely on the view that we are born with some essential part of our mind or psyche that makes us human and in some way shapes who we are and who we become. Some of the influences upon our developing self come from internal psychological development and other influences come from the particular experiences that we had when we were growing up. We also learn a great deal about our self through interactions in adulthood – at work, particularly as we go up the hierarchy, and at home as we become wives, lovers and mothers. The important thing is to spend some time considering and reconsidering who you are.

## Choice and preference: clues to our self-awareness

We cannot take our 'self' for granted. To know our 'self' we have to work hard. That might seem a bit ridiculous – but it depends how you see it. Wanting to 'have it all' is about getting the most out of your life, it is about being fulfilled and being happy. But we are not all going to be happy in the same way or for the same reasons. The really hard work we all have to do, as individuals, is to decide what will make *us* – the person we really are – fulfilled and happy. In that sense then, having it all, is almost the lazy way out. If we go for everything, become Superwoman, then the filtering process of finding out what we really want, gaining the required self-knowledge, the fear of possible failure and accepting that there will be many things that we never achieve or experience because we have chosen not to do them, might be painful. But we all have to make serious choices if we are to be emotionally and physically healthy. Those choices are between personal fulfilment, through self-awareness and knowledge, and the possible annihilation of our 'self' as we relentlessly try to have it all.

## What do we need? What do we want?

There are some basic requirements in life, without which most people would find it difficult to reach a sense of personal fulfilment and happiness. When we see news coverage of the plight of refugees or earthquake victims in Afghanistan, Iraq or Turkey, it is clear that their concerns are *not driven by the need to have it all*. They want simply to survive. They are fleeing for their lives and to secure a future and safety for their children. When we see the images of drought and disease throughout Africa and hear stories of families walking hundreds of miles to find water, food and medicines, we are clear that the mothers who try in vain to suckle their starving infants are not thinking about the perils of being a Superwoman. We need to be able to have food and economic security, health and a sense of personal safety *before* we can give any attention to the more sophisticated needs of self-fulfilment and material wealth that are characteristic of the needs of the aspiring Superwoman.

The psychologists Abraham Maslow[3] and Carl Rogers[4] brought some of these ideas into the public consciousness. Maslow, whose work sounds rather old-fashioned now, was writing during the 1960s when the emphasis, particularly in the USA, was upon self-exploration and the development of human potential. At that time there appeared to be basic resources, safety and food enough for all. To find fulfilment therefore, people searched *inwards* for self-knowledge rather than *outwards* to material comforts.

The fundamental idea of the inner-directed searching as proposed by Maslow was that once the means for physical survival were secured – for instance, food, shelter, health and so on – an individual would then seek their *psychological security* and self-understanding in order to fulfil their potential in life. Moreover, for some people, their need for self-actualisation and self-fulfilment was so great, failure to try and failure to achieve would result in mental and physical ill-health. They would experience emptiness and frustration.

## Fulfilment and health

To quote Maslow:

> *My question was, what made people neurotic?*
> *Where does neurosis come from? And it has also*
> *turned out to be instructive to ask where do fully*
> *human, psychologically sound people come from? Or*
> *even, what is the fullest height to which the human*
> *being can attain? And what prevents him\* from*
> *attaining it?*
>
> *My conclusion was, speaking very generally,*
> *that neuroses, as well as other psychic illnesses,*
> *were due primarily to the absence of certain grati-*
> *fications (of objectively and subjectively perceivable*
> *demands and wishes). These I call basic needs and*
> *called them instinctoid because they had to be*
> *gratified or else illness (or diminution of humanness,*
> *i.e. loss of some of the characteristics that define*
> *humanness) would result. It was implied that*
> *neuroses were closer to being deficiency diseases*
> *than had been thought. And it was further hypothe-*
> *sised that health is impossible unless these needs are*
> *gratified.*[5]

I have quoted Maslow at length here, as I believe that he
raises some important issues for women today. He was
writing as a therapist and academic humanistic psychologist at a time when women were invisible in the discipline
and in society, beyond their roles as mother, housewife

---

\* 'Him' is the word that Maslow and most of his contemporaries used
  for a person! Women were invisible in those days.

and sexual partner. However, he was writing at a period in history also when men (at least in Western societies) were comfortable, powerful and wondering what more they could achieve in their lives. As a consequence of feminist thought and pressure, economic affluence and the widespread expectation of education and achievement throughout industrial societies, it is now *women* who have a need to fulfil themselves. If we follow Maslow's arguments further, we find that there is a complicated psychological phenomenon associated with the Superwoman Syndrome and the desire to have it all. That phenomenon extends beyond the popular rhetoric. Reading the studies he carried out on what he called 'self-actualising' people, we can see that wanting to achieve your full human potential for some of us is almost a necessity of life, similar to food and drink. As Maslow suggests:

> *Self-actualising people are without one single exception, involved in a cause outside their own skin, in something outside of themselves. They are devoted, working at something that is very precious to them – some calling or vocation in the old sense – some priestly sense. They are working at something to which fate has called them to somehow and which they work at and which they love, so the work–joy dichotomy in them disappears.*[6]

If Maslow is correct, then we need to understand Superwoman's motivation as being not so much about mindless 'greed' or selfishness, but about the search for *health*. Until the 1970s, and even later in many countries, it was difficult for women other than those from wealthy or high-status families to gain an education. And, even then, for many of those women their opportunities in business or the professions were severely limited. Marriage was the most 'popular' choice and that frequently and inevitably led to the housewife and motherhood roles. No wonder that so many women experience depression. No wonder that femininity and mental ill-health are seen as being so closely linked. Women's lives and natural ambitions for their emotions and intellect have been systematically curtained over the years. 'Liberation', in the form of educational and professional opportunities, therefore, offers new potential for joy and health, just as with the men that Maslow has written about. But what is the impact of the need to achieve self-fulfilment or actualisation upon our lives? How do we move effectively from being emotionally and intellectually thwarted and constrained to achieving self-actualisation that enables peace, joy and fulfilment?

## Self-actualisation and psychological type

Rowan Bayne,[7] has studied the idea of psychological type and life choices for a number of years. Type theory emerged from the humanistic tradition where the focus of psychology was to enhance self-knowledge and value one's self and others. The work that Bayne and increasing numbers of other psychologists, therapists and management consultants focus upon is the work of Isabel Myers who developed a theory of personality encapsulated in the Myers–Briggs Type Inventory – popularly known as the MBTI. Type theory has three general aims – to do with *self*, *others* and *self-development*. This means:

1   To help people to identify or confirm the ways in

which they – and their 'type' of person – are likely to be most effective and most fulfilled.

**2**  To help people understand and value others more, particularly those who are very different in 'type' from them.

**3**  To help people understand key aspects of the development of their personality throughout life.

At the heart of type theory is the concept of 'preference': that is, a choice we make about doing something that makes us feel most comfortable rather than something that is against our *natural* sense of who we are. Rowan Bayne clarifies this by using the analogy of handedness. Catching a ball with one hand is easy while with the other it is uncomfortable and awkward. He further illustrates the point in the following way:[8]

| **Preferred hand** | **Non-preferred hand** |
| --- | --- |
| Comfortable | Awkward |
| Natural | Clumsy |
| Easy | Childlike |
| Flowing | Much harder |
| Automatic | Timid |
| Confident | Slow |
| | Wobbly |
| | Hard to concentrate |
| | Embarrassing |

If you transfer the idea of handedness preference to behaviour preference, it becomes easy to see how powerful the idea of preference can be. For those whose preference is to make motherhood and the home their primary choice, taking on the additional burden of career achievement is not necessarily self-enhancing. Doing something as hard as managing a career and all that that entails when you would prefer to be putting your main energies into home life can be possible, but difficult and uncomfortable. *It can wear you out and reduce any sense of reward you might have either from your home life or from your work.*

A further perspective on the idea of preference, derives from the work of Carl Rogers who addresses the idea of distinguishing between 'real' and 'false' preferences. In other words, some of our preferences emerge from the kind of person we were born as and became, and are therefore easy or natural. Other preferences are acted upon because of the person we have somehow *thought we ought to be*, and these are false and therefore difficult preferences for us. Rogers' work focuses us upon a self-actualisation of the *real self*, rather than the *false self*. For Rogers the therapeutic journey is initially to discover who we really are, and then to engage in the process of self-actualisation. This is different from the experience of having it all simply because I can! This is about being a Superwoman because I am bright, energetic and have opportunities to prove myself.

## Superwomen, choices and having it all

Today's Superwoman has so many choices. Superwoman can become anything she wants to be: a mother, wife, lover, career-success, feminine, sexy, influential in the community, influential in her profession – and have a social life in addition. The world is there for the taking. That sounds wonderful – the possibility of having it all reverberates with images of opportunities and dreams fulfilled. But beneath the surface of the vision lie pitfalls. The pitfalls are in ourselves if we try to go against what is easy and natural for us as individuals. Pitfalls also exist outside ourselves. Opportunities are often accompanied by anxiety, pressure, stress and fears of failure. Being successful leaves you at the mercy of other people's envy and envy can destroy. To cope well with being Super- woman you have to really know who you are, or have a strong sense of identity and self-knowledge.

The paradox though, is that it is often the failure to know who we are that makes us chase the Superwoman image – which is, at its core, a myth. We think that having it all will give us a secure sense of self and our power and strength will be apparent to others as well. But conversely and perhaps perversely – having it all does not allow us to carve out our sense of self or focus on what we really want for *ourselves* rather than others.

## I know who I am

We exist, operate and experience the world on a number of dimensions as is becoming clear. We have a particular personality type, we have preferences and needs that relate to our type. We also have histories and experiences that are unique to each of us.

Here I want to look at *personal experience*. What *happens to us* psychologically and what are the *psycho- logical effects* of what happens to us while trying to have it all. I also want to ask questions about how personal experience relates to our sense of self and to explore why self-confidence, high self-esteem and having it all are *not* part and parcel of the same experience.

We have all met people who seem totally at ease with themselves. They are not always 'high-flyers' and they are frequently not beautiful, but they have a quality that shines out that makes you wish you could have some of what they have got. But what is it? Beverly works in a bank. She is 37, has two children at primary school, is married to Geoff whom she met at university and she has just been made an assistant branch manager. There are a high proportion of women working at that level, although ten years ago that would not have been the case. Beverly is not a role model for Superwoman, and might even stand accused by Superwomen of being 'ordinary' and unambitious.

So why mention her? One way of describing Beverly might make her look rather smug – because she is clearly happy. She is comfortable with what she can do in the time available to her at work and at home. She is confident that Geoff and she spend time talking about their domestic arrangements, and their family and social lives are important to them both. They are not wealthy but live well and within their means; and both Beverly and Geoff consider that their quality of life has been an improvement on that of their parents. That makes them feel secure and content to live and enjoy the days as they come.

Beverly, though, has not had it easy and has had to make some very serious decisions in the past. Her mother died of cancer when Beverly was 12 years old and she missed out on schooling through caring for her father and younger brother. Her father remarried a woman who did not get on with Beverly and so she went, with her brother, to live with her aunt. She loved and still loves her father but in those early years after his remarriage felt very betrayed. She was also angry with her mother who had left her in that terrible situation.

What made the difference for Beverly was that her aunt made sure that Beverly understood that she was

loved and valued. She made sure that Beverly and her
father kept their relationship intact and her aunt gave
time and attention to Beverly's feelings about betrayal
and abandonment by both of her parents. Her aunt
was prepared to listen to what might to some, including Beverly, seem to be dangerous feelings and to allow
Beverly to see and experience these as legitimate. Beverly
was lucky. What happened to her could easily have made
her afraid that she would be betrayed and abandoned
in many other situations by those she trusted and loved.
She might also have felt guilty about having those feelings. She might have felt the need to flee from those
feelings, anxieties and fears, to punish others, to get her
own back and to find a way of having it all so she never
need feel that she had lost everything ever again. She
probably did, but was helped to recognise the feelings
she had and deal with them *in their context* rather than
become overwhelmed.


## What have feelings got to do with it?


Understanding your feelings – recognising them when
they arise, attributing them appropriately and accepting
them as part of yourself – represents a large component of
what you are like. We are made up of many other things as
well but it is our *feelings* that mediate between aspects of
our self in dynamic ways. It is the feelings that can be
unpredictable and irrational and lead us where we
shouldn't go. In order to know ourselves we need to
know our feelings.

Self-confidence comes from self-knowledge. From
that self-knowledge or awareness we can make choices
that lead to fulfilment in our lives. Striving to have it all

and become today's Superwoman is usually based upon unrealistic judgements about what is best for us as individuals. We may need to have it all because we are unconsciously avoiding an inner lack of awareness or, more frighteningly, a feeling of emptiness. Sometimes we may feel that only by having it all, by being acknowledged by others and seeing ourselves as Superwoman are we able to have a sense of who we are. But of course that is a sham.

Human psychology is complex and contradictory. The psychology of the Superwoman is especially so because she is a relatively new phenomenon, a creation of the late 20th and 21st centuries – post-feminist and New Age. Today's Superwoman is oblivious, or deliberately dismissive, of the struggles that her mothers' contemporaries had for emancipation from the constraints of the male-dominated work place. Today's Superwoman believes that her achievements are unrelated to anything beyond her self and her immediate experiences. Thus she takes her opportunities for granted.

She is also caught up in the fast lane and all its expectations – high achievement, no time for doubt or reflection, the drive towards self-perfection and no room for failure. This contemporary 'psychology' predominates in all the media messages that young women receive. These are not only about movie stars and their magical lives and personal qualities. The messages are all around us – constantly. We hear that exam grades achieved are better than ever before. Everyone has the opportunity to go to university to study for a degree. With relative ease young women can earn more money than their parents' generation. The young also know that they no longer have jobs for life and that in order to make their way in the world and be a success, they need to pass quickly and effortlessly through each stage of their career. Politics and politicians shore up this view. Politics is no longer a site of debate, struggle and contemplation either. It is about certainty and smooth presentation and consensus. There is no time to consider personal philosophy or ideological dilemmas – the message is 'don't waste time on deliberation, get on with the action'.

Thinking about yourself and your needs are, it appears, surplus to contemporary requirements for the successful Superwoman. Counselling and psychotherapy are for those who have become traumatised as a result of terrible events in their lives. It helps them move on. Self-knowledge is an apparently unnecessary luxury. Fitness and health can be achieved through other kinds of thera-pies – physical therapy, reflexology, yoga, shopping and visits to the hairdresser. Looking good and feeling good are vital. But feeling good is not about contemplation and psychological work. As one young woman put it to me, 'I can't stand these people who are constantly picking over the entrails. What do they think they'll find – they need to get on with their lives.'

# Mind the gap!

Feelings and emotions move us forward whether we like it or not. They are the fuel that lubricates the rest of our mind – our intellect, reason, perceptions and personality. Emotions and feelings link the unconscious mind to the conscious mind or sense of self. But for those of us who want to deny the irrational and emotive aspects of our mental lives because they get in the way, threaten our well-being and plague us with doubts when we should be feeling on top of the world – we need to watch out. Whether we like it or not, our emotions are part of us. We have to pay attention or we may fall down the space between our rational and irrational beings. The

psychologist and psychotherapist Dorothy Rowe, talks
about the 'gaps' that are present in many people's
accounts of their lives. Some of these gaps are caused by
a failure to take account fully of what we really want and
where our emotions might be leading us:

> *For a story to be meaningful it must have a begin-
> ning, a middle and an end, and one part must
> connect in a meaningful way to the next.*
>
> *Over my years as a therapist many people have
> told me stories that do not have these criteria of
> meaningfulness. ... They have only talked of an
> unhappy past and an even more unhappy future,
> while the present, the middle of the story, is some-
> where they cannot be. Yet if we cannot live in the
> present we cannot live anywhere, for the present is
> all that we really have.*[9]

Living in the present means we have to be in touch with
ourselves. Living in the present is not the same as living
for the moment. And living for the moment is very different in sentiment from the idea of being *comfortable* in
the present. Daisy had it all but wanted it to be better.
She lived in London with her husband and their children
Stephen and Leonie who were both under five. She had a
successful career by the time she was in her early thirties,
managing an art gallery. She knew many people and had
friends that she saw most nights. She loved her home and
spent a great deal of money on designers and furnishings.
But most of her enjoyment came from the social life
associated with her work. She decided to buy her own
gallery and went into partnership with a man she had met
through work. Shortly Daisy left her husband to live with
this other man. She still considers that she had made all
the right decisions, but she coped with the acrimonious

divorce, child care, financial issues and other pressure on her life by relying on her very supportive (and fortunately affluent and generous) mother – and alcohol. The alcohol, she said, prevented her from having to think and more importantly *feel* what she was losing. She didn't have to go through any sense of doubt because there were these two safety nets always there for her. Daisy coped with the transition, but she was drained and exhausted by the experience. Like Beverly she was lucky in the support she received. But stifling feelings – whether they are feelings of pain or joy – is exhausting.

Feelings are also exhausting if you are letting yourself be overrun by them. Donna became so angry at work because her boss was always trying to control what she was doing, despite the fact that she had gained the relevant professional qualifications and the work itself was well within her capabilities. One day she became so angry that she slammed the door of his office shouting that she was resigning. Half-an-hour later she could not believe what had happened – she had no recollection of where the anger had come from. She had not seen it coming and it exploded upon the situation completely out of her control. It belonged for the most part, to her past life. But the situation she had been in at the time with her boss was a trigger that ignited not only irritation with his behaviour, but the powder keg of her unconscious.

The fact of our personal psychological and emotional history is inescapable for each one of us. We all have a psychological legacy and, if we fail to explore and take account of it, we won't have the strength to withstand the negative forces with which we will doubtless be faced on several occasions over the course of our lives. If we are comfortable with our emotions, we are at ease with our 'self'. All of us benefit *from* taking time to *think* each time we *feel*.

## Self-fulfilment and the emergence of our personal Superwoman

Being out of touch with our emotional life can leave a gap or, more accurately, a sense of emptiness, which many of us fill with achievement and the rewards that that provides. Being a top lawyer, whose experience and expertise is in demand by clients, colleagues and national institutions, gives a clear sense that you are somebody – not just anyone, but someone special – and you can *describe yourself* in terms of *what you do, have done* and *achieved*. But it is frequently the case that some of us find it difficult to be anything else. Who are we when we are not that successful, professional person? Superwoman tries to fill such gaps in her life by being equally involved and active with her partner, children and friends. What today's Superwoman often fails to attend to is *what she actually wants herself rather than what she thinks she ought to want*.

## What others do to you

Usually when we start out on the path to fulfilment with the dream of having it all we are young and unaware of the knocks and rough-and-tumble of the workplace and the home and trying to run both at once. Young women rarely have the in-built self-confidence to tackle (what is still) the male-dominated world of work and power head-on. Self-confidence comes with achievement, but it also takes time and work to gain and maintain it in an appropriate way. Most of us are *vulnerable* because none of us had perfect parents. Perfect parents would have nourished our bodies and our minds consistently enough to make us have the continual sense that we are valued, whatever we do or fail to do. Many of us feel worthy and valued enough, but when things go against us, and we feel the strain for prolonged periods, our vulnerability and self-doubts can be overwhelming. Sometimes they are so overwhelming that we flee. We give up or go under. We cannot cope, become overwhelmed with anxiety, become depressed and panicky. Under these circumstances, when we feel particularly small, lost, forgotten, unloved and unnoticed we try to turn to others for support and reassurance. But for many Superwomen this may be difficult – how do you admit to others you are vulnerable when you cannot bear to think it for yourself? Self-fulfilment requires that we manage the outside attacks, that we build up confidence based on knowledge of *what we are really like* and able to achieve. From that comes a confidence that is not so easily shaken. So how do we understand ourselves better?

## Being confident in adversity

When they arrive on their magic carpet, at the entrance of the academy, profession or organisation of their choice, most women have no idea what lurks in wait for them as they enter. Why should you? The potential and aspiring Superwoman is unlikely to have had any previous experience of being knocked back. To enter what were previously male bastions of power you have had to work long and hard, and successfully. Parents, teachers and friends will have been encouraging and will have recognised and supported your academic strengths.

Entrance to good universities to study subjects such as medicine is still highly competitive. Although in the USA, Canada and the UK there has been a positive effort to make places open to women, the grades needed for entry are still high. Active encouragement of women to enter the course or the profession does not guarantee equal opportunities or support on the way up the hierarchy or even during training.

A few years ago, a male colleague and I did a study of women medical students and junior doctors. These were women who had excelled at school and were doing well at university and quite rightly, dreamed of a glittering career in hospital medicine. They also wanted a family life and a reasonable amount of happiness in their world. In fact their dreams were identical to the young men with whom they were training. We were interested in how they coped in the male-dominated medical profession, what they managed well and how they dealt with the pitfalls. We also traced their expectations of themselves and their futures.

We were not surprised to discover that young women had a hard time – not because they failed exams; not even because they failed to get their feet on the first rungs of the career ladder. In fact they probably did this more successfully than their male counterparts. What shocked them was the hostility and sexism they encountered. Jokes were made about their bodies and general appearance – this happened whatever they looked like. They were taunted for being either too good-looking or not good-looking enough. One told me that a senior doctor, who was in charge of one of her clinical attachments, spoke to his colleague deliberately within her hearing saying 'lovely face, shame about the body'. Another young woman, undertaking a spoken practical exam which involved the examination and diagnosis of a patient, was told off by the examiner in front of the patient and other students. The examiner (a senior middle-aged medical consultant) said that her diagnosis was incorrect and she should spend less time 'in front of the make-up mirror and get on with your work or just go home and have children'. The male students also made some mistakes in their answers, but the response was very different, focusing on what they needed to learn to improve their performance. Both of these women reported these incidents as shaking their confidence so much that they were no longer considering a career in hospital medicine and had decided to become family practitioners instead. Whether that was the right decision in their case does not matter. What is important is that women's self-confidence, particularly as they embark upon their careers, often revolves around their proven academic or work-related capacities. They have not tried themselves out in the professional jungle. They haven't had experience of a world in which you eat or get eaten.

That is only the beginning. When we look at the facts and figures of those organisations and careers that women have been entering for over 20 years, we still see the inequities.

## Conclusions

Women have opportunities in the 21st century that they have never had before. Women have choices and for the first time ever can choose whether they wish to live alone or with a partner of either sex, have children or not and have a career or not. None of these options is easy. Living with other people, negotiating a career or being a reasonable parent all have potential hazards. The hazards come from within and without us – we live in a world with cultural and social expectations and pressures. We inhabit our 'self' which has responded to the rigours of the outside world from birth. We are part of this world and the product of our families. We are therefore not perfect and all vulnerable in different ways. Women as a group have very particular vulnerabilities and hazards that they share in addition to their individual characteristics. Those who aspire to have it all and achieve Superwoman status have particular needs and vulnerabilities. It is likely that they are both special and competent people who need to achieve to be healthy as well as having something to prove as a legacy from earlier assaults on their self.

# Myth, magic or just hard work

*What type of Superwoman are you?*

The Superwoman myth has an impact on all our lives – women feel they have to live up to her or reject her. There seems to be no way of achieving a happy coexistence. Superwoman is the self-imposed standard that exists for us all, whether we are high-flyers or the kind of woman who says 'I'm *only* a secretary'. Whoever you are, you know you have to do it all to have it all. Some women, who may not be the first to spring to mind when you mention 'Superwoman', are truly amazing in their strength and personal resolve to have it all and to achieve through major effort.

Kim was diagnosed with multiple sclerosis, a chronic disabling disease of the central nervous system which leads to deterioration in physical capacity, two years before I met her. Her partner of three years, and father of her two very young children, left her a week after the diagnosis was confirmed. He said he couldn't bear to see her deteriorating over future years – and apart from sending presents for the children at birthdays and Christmas that was the last contact she had with him. Kim was initially traumatised and heartbroken. However, as time passed she realised that she needed to regain her pre-parent and pre-diagnosis life as far as she could. Her disease was of the remitting kind, which meant that although there was a gradual decline in her ability to co-ordinate her muscles and her brain, she could manage at least for the foreseeable future to return to full-time work as a maths teacher. Fortunately for Kim she had no mort-gage to pay on her house and her mother looked after her children during the working day. Even so Kim wanted to be sure that her children did not suffer any more than they had done already with a disappearing father and a disabled mother. She endeavoured to be there for her children when she wasn't at work – to play with them and stimulate them as much as she could, as well as deal with their physical needs such as being bathed and fed. On top of this, which in itself would seem a great deal for a single, disabled parent to deal with, she was a champion chess-player, and continued to play in national competitions.

Another woman, Fallon, who didn't conform to the Superwoman stereotype, also demonstrated amazing abil-ities. She had come from a working-class family in the East End of London. She was fifty when I met her, and had become a Superwoman relatively late in her life. She had been both sexually and physically abused by her father for several years from around the age of eleven until she left school and home at sixteen. She left London and went to work in Dublin as an au pair, where she had a relationship with the father of the chil-dren she was caring for – Eric, a widower. He was in a business partnership with his brother in a small chain of bookshops, and Fallon began to work for them part-time when his children started school. Fallon and Eric even-tually set up home together formally, married and had two more children. Eric died suddenly of a heart attack in his early fifties, but having made sure that Fallon inherited a share of the business. Her talents and energy seemed to be unlocked by his death, even though they had had a successful marriage. She brought up her children and developed the business, which coincided with the rise in the fortunes of Dublin as a vibrant European city throughout the 1990s. Fallon became a well-known figure in the city because she also became involved in charity fund-raising for abused children. From her terrible start in life, she emerged wanting and able to have it all.

# Are you sure you should be doing this?

What has been written about Superwomen over recent years can be supportive – much of it recognising the enormous effort and talents that Superwomen have shown. However, there is another strand to the media and other popular descriptions – the counterattack on Superwoman emerging from some religious and men's groups. For instance:

> *Millions of women are caught in the Superwoman Syndrome and are role-modelling this way of life to others. Some don't recognise they're in this trap; others are trying to free themselves; still others are desperately trying to avoid getting enmeshed. Women with self-esteem issues are at higher risk for getting stuck in this syndrome.*[1]

The image is one of women out of control – out of both society's and their *own* control. The extract above forms the introduction to a religious-based 'exposé' of the

Superwoman Syndrome written in 2001 for 'audiences who want to learn more about avoiding and/or recovering from the Superwoman Syndrome'. Here, being a Superwoman is portrayed as a 'trap' in which women become 'enmeshed'. It is described rather as an *addiction* to alcohol or drugs. Moreover, there is the hint of *psychological inadequacy* in those women who want to achieve in the form of 'self-esteem issues'.

Another internet piece, by Robert Uhlig[2] written in the same year, titled 'Superwoman's weakness exposed', appears on a web site headed with the logos '*da\*di*', '*Dads have the Right Stuff*' and '*Family Matters*'. The article focuses upon a report of research by David Meyer, a professor of psychology at the University of Michigan, who has claimed (quite reasonably I suspect) that we are more efficient when we do one thing at a time. He is quoted in the article as saying: 'In most real-world circumstances you are better off concentrating on a single task for an extended time rather than switching back and forth.' Then he is paraphrased saying that for each aspect of human performance – perceiving, thinking or acting – the brain's executive control, located in the prefrontal cortex and the parietal cortex, has to establish priorities among tasks and allocate the mind's resources accordingly. Meyer gives the example that driving and using a mobile phone is dangerous because the brain is not fully engaged with the driving. This is totally reasonable and not particularly outstanding as a psychological finding. What is worrying though is that the internet article takes the opportunity, based on this research, to attack career women.

*A study reveals today that attempting several tasks at once is inefficient and could even be dangerous. The findings challenge the notion of women 'having it all' as epitomised by the experiences of Shirley Conran and Nicola Horlick.*

*Conran, who wrote a book called Superwoman advising women how to co-ordinate different aspects of their lives, was a designer, artist, journalist and blockbuster novelist, while bringing up a family. She founded Mothers in Management to help professional women juggle their time effectively.*

*Horlick achieved fame four years ago as the mother of five who was head of pension fund management at Morgan Grenfell Asset Management and earned more than £1 million a year.*

*Despite their example, the study claims that because of the way the brain manages responsibilities and tasks doing one thing at a time is usually quicker.*

The remainder of the article says nothing more than what the psychologist was quoted as saying about the brain and doing more than one thing at a time. In no sense did the *psychology professor* mention women juggling home and work. So what is happening? Why are Superwomen getting attacked? And why is there an apparent market for those seeking 'recovery'?

## Describing Superwoman

Superwoman *the myth* is the woman of perfection. She is talented, beautiful and flawless in every way – she chooses to do it all, have it all and, if she fails, it is not to do with her lack of talent or virtue. The rest of us, though, are the other kinds of Superwomen. If we manage to juggle our time, relationships and resources successfully for even short amounts of time, we succeed through magic, luck, or extremes of effort. This often means that we are running on empty – burning our energy stores above and beyond our danger-levels almost all of the time. However, it also means that we are achieving some, or even much, of what we want from life and *putting a great deal back into life as well*!

Superwoman of the latter kind attends to others as well as herself and through wanting to *have it all* (or as much as she can) she may be at risk of losing sight of her self. The everyday Superwoman is an expert in *multitasking* – she can (and has) to do several things at once, and to a reasonably acceptable standard. Time is so tight that there is little available for a second go at things. This requires phenomenal expertise and energy – concentration on complex and routine tasks at the same time. That means: discussing homework with your children, while emptying the dishwasher and writing the shopping list; planning a meeting agenda, while going through your appointments with your secretary and dealing with your nanny's queries on your daughter's health on the telephone.

Superwoman needs help to understand herself and her own needs. She might make *false choices* because she is out of touch with what she wants – all consideration of self having disappeared in the constant round of work at home and in the office. Some commentators argue that this is *the normal state of being a woman* – perhaps all women are 'Superwoman' to some degree or another. One type of ready advice is to:

*Learn to form the following word, 'No!' – 'I don't have time' – 'I have other plans' – and – 'No, there is no age requirement for using a washing machine!'*

> *... Yes, depression is caused by looking at models in magazine ads ... Reassure yourself 'No' they really do not look like that. They are air-brushed clothed – pinned, girdled, ... and starving to death. ... Accept it! You cannot – repeat – cannot make 'everything okay for everyone!' ... If you hear the words 'No problem. I'll take care of it ...', be sure they are being uttered by another woman.*[3]

The message is – accept yourself and your limitations – of time, energy and genes. To accept yourself, though, you need to know yourself. Knowing yourself comes from taking the time to reflect, consider yourself and to know what you want.

Seeking answers to this brings us back to Carl Rogers' idea of the real and false 'self' and issues about self-awareness discussed by Rowan Bayne and Dorothy Rowe in different but complementary ways.

## Real and false choices

The many media images of today's Superwoman, and descriptions of the problems of *doing it all*, exist as constant pressures. On the one hand, if it *is* possible to have it all why not go for it if you have the talent? On the other hand, why on earth put yourself through all that stress, take the risk of failing in everything you do, and end up giving up, like the (apparently) countless others, when the going becomes impossible? We all need a means of self-expression and self-actualisation. We want to make our mark on our world in some way. We want to make the most of our limited time on this earth and find out how we tick. We love life, so let's get the most out of it and the most out of ourselves. Why not? And why not have it all?

## Beware of the false self

What is the false self and why is it dangerous to today's Superwoman? The human experience of being self-aware, while commonplace and part of everyone's experience, is highly complex. Part of this awareness is the drive, motivation or hunger to become what we believe we have the potential to become. That is the process of self-actualisation. That experience of *drive* is real although the *origins* of our motivations may be explained in a number of different ways (e.g. as unconscious drives, as genetic pre-dispositions and as culturally formed responses and so on). As we move forward through our lives we discover those drives that reflect our 'real' self and those that are 'false'. The latter are those that in a variety of ways are the desires of others that we have internalised. They can be in the form of parental or direct social pressure, or internalised social values.

Marilyn loved her father. He had always wanted to train as a lawyer but he was brought up during the Second World War where opportunities for boys from poor families were scarce. He eventually became a teacher, which he enjoyed but desperately wanted more for his daughter than he was able to achieve for himself. Marilyn, however, had a talent for art. She was a brilliant sculptor and gained a scholarship to a famous art school. However, rather than disappoint her father, after much discussion and soul-searching, she studied for and gained entry to law school. She began to believe that this was where she could make her contribution to the world and gain personal satisfaction and indeed she became successful both as a student and as a corporate lawyer. However, she soon got married, had two children and left the law – expressing regret, but arguing that it was the right decision for the sake of her family. As a wife and mother she could argue that she was fulfilling her responsibilities to her family. When her children were older she began sculpting again for pleasure, but she always felt a regret at a deep and not always conscious level, for her missed opportunity to attempt to gain recognition as an artist. She also felt guilty about leaving the law. Through much of her adult life she felt depressed and often angry with her husband and children, although perhaps the real problem for her was following the 'false' self-actualisation which was her father's rather than her own dream.

Women as a group experience social pressure to conform to a broad image of femininity and womanliness. In the 21st century this potentially incorporates career success as well as the domestic achievements of family and relationships. However, within that framework there are clear boundaries that women need to adhere to – they may be imperceptible to some. Women are permitted to be intelligent, but are punished for being too ruthless or competitive, as these attributes are not seen as feminine. Women are now permitted to wear trouser suits to the office but are punished if they are untidy or look unfeminine in some way. Women are seen to be unfeminine if they choose *not* to become mothers or wives. There are certain opportunities that are formally or informally closed to women, partly because of social taboos (for instance women are frequently prevented from being miners or engage in professional boxing), and partly because it is believed that they do not have the physical skills (for example, until recently it was argued that orthopaedic surgeons needed a great deal of physical strength to carry out their work so it was not a suitable career for women).

Women, as human beings like all others, have a sense of what is real for them and what they need to do to fulfil their promise to themselves and the world. But sometimes disentangling the real self is difficult.

## The real self: understanding our drives

The Myers–Briggs Type Inventory (MBTI)[4] has been shown time and again to help individuals and psychologists identify what are fundamental characteristics of the self or personality. The personal profile that we identify from completion of the inventory gives a long-lasting indication of the important characteristics that underlie our preferences and the choices we *should* make in our lives if we are to be self-actualising. Understanding ourselves in this way and recognising that we are different from others in these basic ways that reflect our preferences also has the potential to develop a humanistic tolerance of others in each of us.

We recognise that other people make different choices and have different preferences and skills from us. If we choose to carry out certain options that relate to our preference or type, we are more likely to feel secure and comfortable with ourselves than if we make choices against our type when we will feel clumsy, awkward, out of place and unfulfilled. The MBTI recognises four dimensions or scales that are crucial to understanding the personality type preferences that we reveal. We can all place ourselves somewhere between each of the following extremes along each scale:

| Extraversion (E): | Introversion (I): |
|---|---|
| Prefers outer world of people to inner reflection / active / gaining energy from others / wanting to experience in order to understand / works by trial and error / likes variety | Prefers reflection and inner world / prefers writing to talking / may enjoy social contact but needs personal space to recover / wants to understand something better before trying it / persistent / likes quiet space to work in |
| Sensing (S): | Intuition (N): |
| Likes facts / realistic and practical / observant / works steadily and step by step / enjoys owning things and making them work / patient and good with detail | Sees possibilities and patterns / imaginative and speculative / likes to see overall picture / works in bursts of energy with quiet periods in between (needs inspiration) / likes variety / impatient with routine |
| Thinking (S): | Feeling (F): |
| Fair, firm-minded and sceptical / analytical and logical / brief and business-like / critical / clear and consistent principles | Warm, sympathetic and aware of how others feel / trusting / enjoys pleasing others / needs harmony, clear and consistent values |
| Judging (J): | Perceiving (P): |
| Decisive / industrious and determined / organised and systematic / takes deadlines seriously / likes to have things decided and and settled | Curious / flexible and tolerant / leaves things open / pulls things together well at the last minute / samples many more experiences than can be digested or used |

**Figure 3**   Psychological type.

- 'extraversion' (E) or 'introversion' (I)
- 'sensing' (S) or 'intuitive' (N)
- 'thinking' (T) or 'feeling' (F)
- 'judging' (J) or 'perceiving' (P)

*Extraversion* and *introversion* describe the ways we *feel* about people and *relate* to them. The terms have been used for so long in popular psychology that most people are familiar with them. The common understanding of the introvert is as a shy, retiring person and the extrovert as the party-goer. But, as you can see from Figure 3, there is more to it than that. This dimension of personality also refers to wider aspects of the ways we interact with our

internal as well as our external worlds. Just because you
are shy does not mean you are an introvert. Introverts also
need company. Extroverts manage their working lives in
what introverts might see as a chaotic way, while an extrovert might accuse an introvert of being too pedantic.
An introvert might be seen as a steady, reflective person
who would make a good home-maker or mother because
they don't appear to want lots of company and social
activity in their lives. You could also see, though, that
such a person might find the demands of child care
rather intrusive. An extravert on the other hand, could
be stimulating to children, seek out friends among other
mothers and make an excellent hostess and not miss the
cut-and-thrust of workplace encounters in the least.

*Sensing* and *intuition* are about ways of gathering information. Sensing types attend to sequences and take
things one at a time. They make good scientists. Intuition
types are more likely to gain a quick overview of a situation while jumping from topic to topic. They are also
impatient with routine and are unlikely to cope with a
repetitive office job or the routine chores of housework.
They make good managers and creative writers.

*Thinking* and *feeling* are about different ways of
making decisions and coming to conclusions. Rowan
Bayne makes the point that *thinking* types are often seen
as unemotional. That is not the case. It is simply that
*feeling* types are more likely to use emotions in their
decision-making than thinking types, who tend to solve
problems in a more objective way. The thinking type is
more likely to cope well in debate without getting emotionally involved, particularly if it is about a non-personal
subject, such as deciding about who to employ or to which
company to give a contract.

Characteristically, when making decisions, a feeling
type would pay attention to how the rejected candidate
might feel or which colleagues might make better work-

mates because of their compatibility rather than skills. Again these are differences in preferences, not superior or inferior modes of decision-making. There is some evidence that men and women might differ significantly along this particular dimension: women are more likely to be *expected* to be feeling rather than thinking types. A woman who is a feeling type is more likely to be considered as feminine than one who is primarily a thinking type. Research on stereotypes indicates that thinking women may be seen as aggressive and hard-nosed, unpopular with male peers, and so may pretend to behave in another way in order to avoid being seen thus. Feeling men also have problems because they are generally perceived to be un-masculine or wimps.

*Judging* and *perceiving* refer to the ways in which we understand other people and situations. Judging types prefer to have *all* the information before they decide on a course of action or make a decision. Perceiving types are more likely to act suddenly, when 'the penny drops'.

We will all be able to locate ourselves somewhere along each of these dimensions and, in so doing, gain a sense of what we are like, our 'type' and thus what styles of thinking and behaviour suit us best. Having that information enables effective self-actualisation.

## What about Superwoman?

Superwoman can emerge with any of these type preferences. The question we need to ask ourselves is: how far does our current lifestyle force us to go *against* our type preference, and how much is compatible *with* our preference? As we saw in Chapter 3 with the model of handedness, if you are right-handed and forced to use your left hand, a lot of effort goes into doing most things fairly badly and you end up feeling clumsy, awkward, out of place and, at the end of it, thoroughly exhausted.

Janet, a genetic scientist, worked along with her husband for a pharmaceutical company. They had two young children and she firmly believed in taking main responsibility at home for domestic chores and overseeing child care. She also tried to spend as much time with her children as she could when she was at home in the evenings and at weekends. She had children relatively late in life, her son when she was 39 and her daughter two years later. She loved them dearly and they were much wanted. The difficulty for Janet was that her life had been her work up until late on in her first pregnancy and that was also central to her relationship with her husband. Her psychological type preferences identified her as an introverted (I), sensing (S), thinking (T) and judging (J) type: ISTJ. Now typical I + T characteristics included being high achievers who enjoy complexity, are competitive with their self and others, non-conformist and argumentative. S + J types are decisive, structured, orderly, precise and resistant to change. These qualities suited her admirably for her job as a scientist and as an employee of a demanding company. She had to work long hours. The competition among her colleagues and the race against the clock to market products in time to compete with rival companies was tough. Janet thrived, even though many people found that work and the working environment stressful and highly pressured. Janet managed well, because, on the whole, the demands fitted exactly with her preference type. However, once the children arrived and her sense of duty, her knowledge about the benefits that stimulation and love could bring to children and her sense of social responsibility brought other things to her life. She came to feel that she was falling apart. This was compounded by her love for her children.

But her relationship with her husband had now come to be about making arrangements simply to cope with their lives. It was no longer about the things that interested them both, such as the essence of their work or company politics. It wasn't that she couldn't stand the pace or the demands on her time and attention. It was that the nature of the extra demands ran contrary to what she felt was natural for her. This was the basis of her stress.

Janet had never had reason to get a psychological assessment done of her type – she naturally fitted into the working environment in which she thrived. She was lucky. She had also always wanted and expected to have children. She did not anticipate in any way what children were like or the specific kind of demands that parenthood makes. Her 'real' self was the work-related one and the 'false' self was the child care one. The conflict between the two placed her at risk of giving up and becoming ill.

Karen experienced a very similar type of stress to Janet, but for different reasons. She had never been very ambitious and was happily assessed as NF and SP. She had three children and, although she was a single parent, was never short of company from her many loyal friends. She also had no shortage of offers from potential boyfriends. She was a warm, kind person who trained as a counsellor and worked part-time for a family doctor and part-time as a stress counsellor for a large high-tech manufacturing company. These were very different organisations with different expectations but Karen loved the variety and her training and personality fitted her for both. However, the high-tech company offered Karen a full-time promoted post in which she would have to manage a team of counsellors and get involved in the company's management team. It was exciting and Karen enjoyed the promotion and the prospect of being able to manage a team well. However, the demands were different from those that she had perceived. She was now a manager and had to deal with people in a different way from when she was a counsellor. Karen was now controlling people not helping them. She felt that she was losing her integrity because she used some of her counselling skills to manipulate and expose people in ways that the company demanded and that, she felt, went against the grain. She also had less time and energy for her family and friends. However, she was so good at this new job that a year later she was promoted again, which removed her even further from 'ordinary' people. Her life was now about high-powered meetings, travel, and communicating, usually via her secretary, and she felt overwhelmed by the constant flow of paperwork and emails. Karen was very good at her job but gradually the stress of going against her type put a great deal of stress into her previously happy life and she quit.

Janet and Karen could be seen as failed Superwomen; but I favour the other interpretation which is that, for reasons which were to an extent unforeseen and out of their control, they succumbed to having to spend much of their lives doing things that took up a great deal of their energy because they were not things they would naturally have chosen.

## What kind of Superwoman are you?

Psychological type may change in the course of a person's life, particularly if that person undergoes a fundamental shift in their social environment or belief system due to changes in the context in which they live. However, on the whole, if we are serious about working on our self-actualisation and disciplined and objective in our evaluations, we can identify the kind of Superwoman that we are or will become. From that we can gain a knowledge of

| Career/task focused | Home/relationship focused |
|---|---|
| Trait and behaviour preferences: extreme task-related competence, ability to negotiate career ladder, strategic vision, stamina, ambition | Trait and behaviour preferences: relationship centred, emotional and warm, caring, interested in arts/crafts, creativity |
| Personal qualities: emotional intelligence, competitiveness, good at managing people and stressful situations, feminine, attractive, energetic | Personal qualities: emotional intelligence, ability to 'multitask', gains satisfaction from others' development and growth, feminine, attractive, energetic, cooperative |
| Potential hazards: too much stress, isolation, lack of support, inability to recognise gendered nature of workplace, discrimination | Potential hazards: overload, lack of appreciation, breakdown of the domestic unit, emotional betrayal |

**Figure 4**  Which type of Superwoman are you?

what activities and relationships will be stressful and exhausting and what ones will be nourishing and rewarding. All the discussions about Superwoman, having it all and letting go of various behaviours in order to gain a greater balance in life, focus around the home/work conflict. It is fair to say that regardless of women's specific preference types, it is the strain of career demands and family demands that call our lives into serious question. We usually know what we value in ourselves, if we are prepared to give it a little thought. Some of those attributes are better centred on career and some on domestic life and, although these attributes should not be seen as fixed commodities, it is important for Superwomen who are experiencing stress and dilemmas about what path to choose to identify which type of Superwoman they are at the moment. For each set of characteristics that you claim and recognise as those currently guiding you, there are qualities which relate to your lifestyle that are necessary to enable you to be good at what you have chosen to do. Those same qualities will also be necessary to guide you around the potential hazards that your choice brings.

## But really – who are you?

But there is more to our sense of who we are than personality or preference type, although that clearly provides
important insights into how we handle our lives. We
also have an ongoing relationship with our 'self' in
which we try to engage with our desires, drives, motivations, successes, failures, future identities and feelings.
Our relationship with our self is a close relative of our
preference type, but it takes place in a more chaotic and
emotional way – a fact that doesn't please us all, particularly if we are sensing, thinking, and judging rather than
intuitive, feeling and perceiving.

# The rise of Superwoman

*From fear of success to emotional intelligence*

> *For women, as for certain other groups of people, being oneself – authenticity – was hardly spoken of seriously until recently, although it figured prominently in the concerns of members of the dominant culture.*[1]

> *The modern Mizz has a much harder task ahead of her. Looks are clearly still important, but she also has to have 'personality'.*[2]

> *What are 'masculinity' and 'femininity'? Every society has ways of distinguishing the sexes – socially, culturally, psychologically. Historically, however, the way this division has been drawn has varied enormously. What counts as maleness or femaleness in one period or cultural setting can look radically unlike its equivalents in other times or places. And similarly, how an individual comes to identify him or herself as belonging to a gender also varies greatly.*[3]

*It seems that women have made few contributions to the discoveries and inventions in the history of civilisation; there is, however, one technique which they may have invented – that of plaiting and weaving.*[4]

Only towards the end of the 20th century did Western writers, politicians and academics take women's psychology seriously. Until the late 1960s (and even after then) women were depicted as the 'other', the residual category – the counterpart to men. 'Man' was a word used to represent humankind; but descriptions of 'man' clearly focused on the human male, not men and women. The impact of this has been that we are only now 'discovering' women's psychology – and we still have a long way to go. The academic discipline of psychology had an important influence on 20th century understanding of the family, child development, child-rearing practices, sex roles, education, achievement at school and at work, and on the creation of an 'effective' climate for workplace organisations. Management science, mental health, educational attainment, leadership skills, competition, power and creativity are among the key concepts that have been brought forward into the 21st century as the legacy of psychology.

## Women's motives at work

Among some of the first questions that psychologists and management scientists asked about women at work were questions about motivation, career choice and the professional achievement. Why were women consistently in

junior positions in relation to men colleagues? Were
women able to become competent scientists or engineers?
Did women have the killer instinct that would allow them
to reach the top in business? Women did not seem to be
achieving high positions in the workplace, so perhaps
there was something about women themselves that prevented them from being as successful as men were.

The conclusions that were drawn about women from
research following the Second World War was that they
lacked the motivation to have a successful career. This
work remained largely unchallenged until the late 1960s.

## Fear of success: the *myth* of the passive woman?

Matina Horner, one of the few academic psychologists in
the USA at that time, carried out her own studies to test
the proposition that somehow women *feared success* in the
workplace because they did not wish to be seen as pushy
and unfeminine. That is because, to succeed at work, a
person has to be competitive and that was against popular
ideas of being feminine. However bright and however
ambitious a woman was, she had to prevent herself from
becoming *visibly* successful, otherwise she would be seen
as unfeminine.

Horner carried out her research by using stories about
male and female medical students and their success in
exams and then asking people to explain what happened
to those students and why. She found that her female
respondents, through talking about the students, expressed their own *fear of success* in three main ways:

- a fear of social rejection
- internal, secret personal fears of not being feminine
- an unconscious punishment of and impulse to destroy the woman student who did well in the exams

Horner's work gained publicity and acclaim because it appeared to fit the overwhelming cultural belief that women were their own worst enemies at work. Declarations about her study abounded in the mass media. The conclusion was drawn that there was no workplace discrimination in the USA! Men *do* better at work because they try harder and *are* better!

But that perspective belied what Horner had been trying to say. She demonstrated that women *wanted* to succeed in their careers but *feared they would be punished in some way for doing so*. Thus they fell at the last hurdle and allowed their male colleagues to win. She said:

> *I have suggested that women have a latent personality disposition or a 'motive to avoid success'; i.e. that they becomes anxious because of success. This is not at all the same as saying that they have a 'will to fail', i.e. a 'motive to approach failure'. This would imply that women actively seek out failure because they anticipate or expect positive consequences from failing. The [motive to avoid success], on the other hand, implies that women inhibit their positive achievement directed tendencies because of the arousal of anxiety about the negative consequences they expect will follow success.*[5]

Although the world has changed a great deal since the

1970s as far as women at work are concerned, the need to be feminine as well as a career-Superwoman is still high on the agenda. This presents a dilemma – how can you achieve self-actualisation and avoid being punished for your achievements? Why is something that you are good at and seem suited for, seen by others as unfeminine? Women become paralysed when faced with these irrational criticisms and self-reproaches.

What are the origins of the flurry of Superwomen opting out? Why is this behaviour apparently welcomed by the media and by (some) women? As I looked through the numerous web sites and journalistic accounts of successful women plumping for a lower-grade job so they could devote more time to their family, there was an eerie reverberation with Horner's 'fear of success'. The emphasis was on women being mothers before everything else. While they may try their hand in the corporate world, when it comes to the crunch they return to what suits them best – caring for and nurturing their families.

One story is of a black woman, Felicia Taylor, reported as having won the 6th Annual Tribute to Working Women Award[6] who was also in the process of adopting two of the boys that she and her husband had been fostering (along with her own five boys aged between 4 and 12). She is reported to have said:

> *I felt I could make a difference in their lives ... I love to get up in the morning at 4.30 and fix my family a nice, big hot breakfast before they go out to face the day. It makes me feel good knowing that they can start out each morning well-fed.*

Another Superwoman in flight declared:

> *So take it from me, a chronic Superwoman Syndrome sufferer, let the things that aren't so*

*important go and you'll quickly see that what is left
is more time, enjoyment, and fulfilment for the
things that you treasure.*[7]

And finally:

*You too can return to sanity! 12 steps to ... Super-
woman Freedom!*[8]

The reasons given for 'retreat' seem to be that being
Superwoman is *insane*. Pleasure for women is to be
gained from giving to your family. The message is to
put family first and avoid things such as career politics
that are unimportant by comparison. Surely women
today are not still fearing that their femininity is called
into question if they focus on their careers?

Eleni was an account manager in a public relations
company. The day-to-day environment was busy, exciting and highly competitive. The company had to fight for
business and the teams within the company had to
demonstrate their value in comparison to the other
teams, mostly by the income from accounts they could
win. The senior account manager in her team was losing
his grip on the management of the team. He was spending
too much time socialising with the clients, and was clearly
the worse for wear and suffering from too much alcohol
and too little sleep. Eleni was very concerned as she saw
that the team was suffering. She tried to talk to him. She
disagreed with his decisions and increasingly found
herself speaking out against the way he was handling the
clients and his staff. His behaviour was splitting the team.
He openly favoured some people, and clearly briefed
against Eleni and eventually she became depressed and
unsure what to do. She considered applying for another

job, but she enjoyed the particular one she did. She continued to argue with him but the situation in the team got worse and she became even more concerned and angry and it began to affect her health. One day, though, she decided that enough was enough – there was no point in challenging from the sidelines any more. She made an open declaration of war and challenged him for control of the team. She arranged a meeting with the overall boss, the company director, and her senior manager in which she made it clear that she would be a better person to take over his job. She was allowed to submit a plan for change, which the company director accepted, and she was promoted and her colleague sidelined. Talking later to her male and female friends – none of them could work out why she had not made the direct challenge to take over the team from the start. It was clear that she had a better grasp of the business and how to motivate the team, and she also demonstrated a future vision. Eleni herself wondered why she hadn't. It was, she realised, that she had not wanted to risk being rejected and had not predicted that a challenge for leadership was so easily accomplished and won. To fight to win appeared to be an aggressive and competitive stance, rather than the concerned team member position that she had seen herself in when she was challenging his decision-making.

Psychological research on women and by women over the past 30-plus years continues to suggest that the fear of being thought unfeminine is stronger than the motivation to achieve. The punishment for not being a *proper* feminine woman seems to be so terrifying that it challenges the very core of our identities. It prevents our drive towards self-actualisation. Not being seen as feminine potentially annihilates the female self for Superwoman and this threatened punishment has continued into the 21st century. But what exactly is femininity, how can we recognise it? What are its psychological origins?

## Femininity and passivity: women's natural self?

Freud among other psychoanalysts had a great deal to say about the nature of femininity and issued some dire warnings to those women who attempted to 'imitate' men. He was very clear that there were distinct psychological and behavioural differences between the sexes, which had their roots in biology and 'nature'.

> *You cannot give the concepts of 'masculine' and 'feminine' any new connotation. The distinction is not a psychological one; when you say 'masculine', you usually mean 'active', and when you say 'feminine' you usually mean 'passive'.*[9]

The idea of women and femininity being equivalent to passivity is not new. The Bible and medieval myths of knights, fairies, dragons and ladies in distress all serve to confirm that contemporary notions of femininity have their roots deep within a culture that sees men as superior. We have to hide our drives and success if we are not to get punished and destroyed.

In contemporary Western society we place science above myth and most Superwomen as part of this culture probably agree with this hierarchy. Science is objective, true and based on reality, and gives a clear meaning to our lives. However, psychological and medical science have a history of saying things about men and women that contradict the potential *existence* of Superwoman, and many of their values are embedded in our collective consciousness. Science has sown, and continues to harvest, women's seeds of self-doubt and dependency.

- considerate
- gentle
- cries more easily
- understanding of others
- aware of others' feelings
- interested in appearance
- feelings easily hurt
- passive
- able to devote self
  to others

- hides emotions
- dominant
- assertive
- reckless
- intelligent
- logical
- sloppy
- aggressive
- competitive
- active

**Figure 5**  Stereotypes of femininity and masculinity.

It was only relatively recently that psychologists recognised that women and men held similarly stereotypical views about the differences between the qualities of each sex. Psychologists working in the 1970s and 1980s showed that most of us believed that there were marked character differences between women and men and that these also described the core of normal masculinity and femininity. Thus men were seen to be aggressive, competitive, independent, assertive, logical; and women as passive, dependent, less intelligent and illogical. The characteristics of men equipped them for leadership, power and success and those of women equipped them to be good wives and mothers. So what are the origins of these immutable beliefs about gender differences?

## Different bodies, different minds

*When you meet a human being, the first distinction you make is 'male or female?' and you are accustomed to make the distinction with unhesitating certainty.*[10]

But why should men and women be so different from each
other? For the answers, psychology has focused on the
relationship between the body and the mind. One of the
most conspicuous and influential theories is that of
psychoanalysis. Here the body's sexual development has
been used to support the idea of the *naturally passive
woman*. The differences between the male and female
body are usually obvious, and this is accentuated
through the way the individual is dressed and how they
hold, move and generally control their physical presence.
Psychoanalysis, more than any other approach to psychology, links the body with the mind/emotions and the social
realms of sex/gender.

## Freud and femininity

> *Throughout history people have knocked their heads
> against the riddle of the nature of femininity ...
> Nor will you have escaped worrying over this
> problem – those of you who are men; to those of
> you who are women this will not apply – you your-
> selves are the problem.*[11]

Freud's comprehensive view of sex/gender is as follows.
The human psyche comprises a three-part structure – the
*ego*, the *superego* and the *id*. The infant is born with the id
in place, which is the source of unconscious instincts and
drives. During the first year of life the ego (or the self
which links the individual both with other people and
reality) begins to develop, and around the ages of 5–6
the superego or conscience begins to form. Although
girls and boys are born with different genitals, they have

no knowledge of this difference at first. Thus there is little to distinguish them psychologically from each other in their early development.

Psychosexual development occurs through the journey of the *libido* (the main source of emotional energy which is an instinctual drive) through the body's erogenous zones in sequence as they each in turn become the site of developmental energy: the mouth, the anus and the genitals. The stages of development that we pass through are in an age-related sequence and each is named according to the focus of the libidinal energy:

- oral stage (from birth until around 12 months)
- anal stage (up until the age of 2–3 years)
- phallic stage (up until the age of 4–5 years)
- latency (around the ages of 5–6 years)
- genital stage (up to and beyond adolescence)

The developmental sequences can be seen through observation of infants as they develop. For example their early engagement with the world involves stimulation of the lips and mouth – feeding and later sucking their thumbs and fingers. This is followed by the anal stage during which the infant can be observed gaining pleasure from bowel activity or withholding bowel movements as their parent is potty training them. Their attention then turns to genital stimulation at the phallic stage at around the ages of four and five. Here the differences between girls and boys become more easily recognised and it is from this stage onwards that their psychologies *diverge* and gender-related characteristics begin to form.

Underlying the process of psychosexual development for the infant boy is the *unconscious* belief that everyone has a penis, which he realises is very valuable to him. It is the discovery that not everyone *does* have one, that girls do

| The boy | The girl |
|---|---|
| ● Masturbates at the phallic stage | ● Masturbates, wants mother for herself and sees the father as her rival |
| ● Wants mother for himself and sees father as rival | |
| ● Sees sister as castrated | ● Sees brother's penis |
| ● Gives up on his mother and identifies with his father | ● Envies the penis |
| ● The fear of castration is so great that the boy forms a strong superego and forms his sexual identity | ● Turns against her mother in shame and anger and turns to her father to have his penis – a baby will eventually be the equivalent for her |
| | ● Develops a weak superego and sexual identity |

**Figure 6**   The Oedipal crisis.

not, that makes him anxious and in fear of *castration*. During the genital stage the boy has unconscious fantasies about sexual desires towards his mother, and believes that his father might recognise these desires and castrate him. To avoid the rivalry and wrath of his father the boy identifies with his father's masculinity positioning himself with all men as different from women. This is the resolution of the Oedipal crisis.

Freud was less decisive in his account of girls' resolution of their sense of lack. The girl recognises that she does not have the valued penis, and turns against her mother who does not have one either. She feels betrayed, but reluctantly identifies with femininity and women. The girl's fantasy during the phallic stage, is sexual desire for the father and her belief that he will supply her with a baby to substitute for the missing penis.

His evidence for the psychological importance of anatomical distinction in different characteristics in women and men is what he calls women's *castration complex*. When girls see the genitals of the other sex they consider themselves to be seriously wronged and fall victim to 'envy for the penis', which will leave 'ineradicable traces' on their development and the formation of their character. For Freud, these ineradicable traces may be seen in a subsequent desire to 'resist' normal femininity by having desires beyond motherhood, particularly those involving an intellectual life and a career. This masculinity complex occurs when the girl continues to behave in an active way into adulthood, the extreme of which he sees as female homosexuality. Normal femininity equals passivity and motherhood. His view that the male is naturally 'active' and the female 'passive' by virtue of their genitals and their function during sexual intercourse, is only contradicted in women's 'active' behaviour in relation to caring for infants/children.

Freud meant all of this literally. However, subsequent feminist scholars have made the point that *the penis has a symbolic meaning* in most societies in that it represents patriarchal/male power. Not having a penis, that is being female, equals being on the political sidelines.

## Biology, genes, brains and gender

More recently a different view of gender differences has been offered by psychologists who address questions of why in particular women seem to be better at child care than men and men have greater career success than women. These explanations arise from what in the 1960s was called sociobiology and is now called evolutionary psychology. As with psychoanalytic explanations of gender differences, it is the extremes that have been adopted by the media and used against women. Edward Wilson, a biologist, originally argued that women and men behave differently and those differences are biologically based and immutable. His approach was grounded

upon Darwinian principles of *natural selection* – which is
the competition for survival. Survival is not only about
survival in the person or animal's own life-time, but it also
involves biological reproduction so that our genes are
passed on. Darwin further identified the importance of
*sexual selection*, through which some individual animals
and humans had advantages over others of the same sex
and species which made them particularly attractive to the
other sex. These attractive qualities were reproduced, as
individuals with these qualities were those most likely to
'mate'.

General sex differences thus arise from sexual selection, because the genes of those most attractive to the
other sex are the ones that are most likely to be reproduced. Women who reproduced were the ones who were
physically strong, able to bear and rear children effectively. Men who reproduced were the ones who were
able to gain access to women. As Anne Campbell[12]
describes it:

> the traits that assist men and women in carrying
> their genes forward are not identical. What is a
> good strategy for a man may be counterproductive
> for a woman. Over evolutionary time we begin to
> see a sex difference appear. Baby girls receive those
> genes that selectively help females to become repro-
> ductively successful while baby boys receive a
> slightly different complement of genes that in the
> past have helped their fathers and grandfathers.
> ... Whatever the pathway used, each sex
> receives the genetic instructions most useful for
> building a mind that will enhance the body's repro-
> ductive success. So sex differences are expected only
> where they have a direct influence on sex-specific
> reproductive strategy. Biology can point to the

*sexual strategies of men and women that lie behind evolved psychological differences.*

The outline of this theory of sexual differences in psychological capacities is based upon Darwinian sexual selection in the context of parental investment. It goes as follows:

**1** Men and women have different levels of investment in each of their offspring.

**2** The more time we devote to reproducing one child, the less time there is available for reproducing others.

**3** A woman can only get pregnant once over the course of her monthly menstrual cycle.

**4** If she succeeds in getting pregnant, then it takes nine months before the child is born; then she has to breastfeed and then look after the child until it is independent enough to survive without her constant attention.

**5** Therefore, to a mother, each baby represents a large investment of time, energy and emotion.

**6** This is not so for a man. He can ejaculate several times a day. A man could probably father around half-a-dozen infants each day.

**7** Psychological differences between the behaviour and psychological attributes of women and men have evolved based on this differential level of investment. Through sexual selection it is those women who are *good mothers* and those men who are prepared to *take risks* challenging other men, and with whom women are prepared to 'mate', whose genes are reproduced.

**8**  Therefore men have evolved to take risks and be assertive and competitive with other men in order to be the ones who get the opportunities to reproduce. Women have evolved to be selective and caring. In other words, *men court* and *women choose* and these kinds of behaviours and ways of thinking about the world get transferred to other activities as well.

Thus men and women interact differently with the world. They behave and understand their family and career worlds differently from each other, although many evolutionary psychologists would argue that evolution and cultural transmission and changes all impact upon the way we behave. As men have had unrestricted power over the world of work for so long, it is therefore no surprise that most organisations operate according to man-made rules and traditions, and it therefore is equally unsurprising that these values are perpetuated through employment and promotion policies.

# From different psychologies to better psychologies

Women and men think about and behave differently in the workplace. It is still not clear whether there are mainly social or biological reasons for these differences, but the differences in styles are obvious. Even the most successful corporate Superwoman achieves her power and communicates differently from the ways of her successful male colleagues. Deborah Tannen[13] begins her classic book about men and women's communication styles at work as follows:

> *Amy was a manager with a problem: she had just read a final report written by Donald, and she felt it was woefully inadequate. She faced the unsavoury task of telling him to do it over. When she met with Donald, she made sure to soften the blow by beginning with praise, telling him everything about his report that was good. Then she went on to explain what was lacking and what needed to be done to make it acceptable. She was pleased with the diplomatic way she had handled the bad news. Thanks to her thoughtfulness in starting with praise, Donald was able to listen to the criticism and seemed to understand what was needed. But when the revised report appeared on her desk, Amy was shocked. Donald had made only minor, superficial changes, and none of the necessary ones. The next meeting with him did not go well. He was incensed that she was now telling him his report was not acceptable and accused her of having misled him. 'You told me before it was fine.'*

Amy's thoughts about diplomacy and good communication seemed equivalent to dishonesty to Donald.

Women find overt aggression difficult to deal with. Freddie was a town planner charged with designing and implementing a traffic scheme around a highly congested suburban dwelling and shopping area. She worked hard,

consulted widely and then arrived at a compromise she
had to present to the local community. As part of her
presentation, she showed that some areas were not to be
developed immediately and there was still scope to work
on the plans, and in this way she wanted to flag that up to
her audience so they might make suggestions and contact
her in her office. She thought she was providing an opportunity for increased democracy, but three local men in
the audience attacked her relentlessly for being sloppy,
unprepared and unwilling to take the initiative. She was
very shaken by their response, because she believed she
was being more than fair to them, by giving opportunities
for choice; but the men thought she wasn't doing her job.

Increasingly there has been a call for more attention at
work to be paid to how relationships are handled and
managed rather than to sheer competitiveness and aggression. This favours women's success.

## Emotional intelligence and female natures: are we the winners now?

*The rules for work are changing. We're being
judged by a new yardstick: not just by how smart
we are, or by our training and expertise, but also by
how well we handle ourselves and each other. This
yardstick is increasingly applied in choosing who
will be hired and who will not, who will be let go
and who retained, who passed over and who
promoted.*[14]

Superwoman will have already discovered that the world
of business, commerce and the professions has increas-

ingly come to value the kinds of skills that are traditionally seen as female ones. In short, companies and organisations are now demanding emotional as well as technical competence in their leaders. Increased business competition, the expansion of the global economy and the high stakes all suggest that the masculine domains of risk and aggression should be to the fore. But that is no longer the case. It has become essential that successful strategies are those that involve medium- to long-term goals. Short-term solutions are no longer effective. We have seen how risk-taking, by individuals such as Nick Leeson, and by investors on the international stockmarkets, can lead to long-term recessions and financial disasters. More considered attention is being given to the quality of an organisation or company – rather than just to a notional valuation of their shares.

Big business and international leadership now require *emotional intelligence* – considered to be central in any professional negotiating activity. This enables you to handle emotionally charged situations more effectively. Such situations include managing people, selling, negotiating, and listening. Emotional competence is in great demand and it is believed that high-flying women have a great deal more of it than many otherwise competent men.

## Emotional competence

Daniel Goleman,[15] a leading author on the subject of emotional intelligence, describes a landmark study of top executives who were 'derailed' – that is lost their jobs or failed to gain the promotions they were expecting. The two most common characteristics of those who failed were:

- *Rigidity*: that is, they were unable to adapt their style to changes in the organisational culture, or they were unable to take in or respond to feedback about traits they needed to change or improve. They couldn't listen or learn.
- *Poor relationships*: they were too harshly critical, insensitive, or demanding, so that they alienated those they worked with.

The successful managers exhibited emotional competence. That included:

- *Self-control*: those who derailed handled pressure poorly and were prone to moodiness and angry outbursts. The successful stayed composed under stress, remaining calm and confident – and dependable in a crisis.
- *Conscientiousness*: the derailed group reacted to failure and criticism defensively – denying, covering up, or passing the blame. The successful took responsibility by admitting their mistakes and failures, taking action to fix the problems, and moving on without ruminating about their lapse.
- *Trustworthiness*: the failures typically were overly ambitious, too ready to get ahead at the expense of others. The successful had high integrity with a strong concern for the needs of their subordinates and colleagues, and for the demands of the tasks at hand, giving the tasks a higher priority than impressing their boss.
- *Social skills*: the failures lacked empathy and sensitivity, and so were often abrasive, arrogant, or given to intimidation of subordinates. While some were charming on occasion, even seeming concerned about others, the charm was purely manipulative.

The successful were empathic and sensitive showing tact and consideration in their dealings with everyone, superiors and subordinates alike.

- *Building bonds and supporting diversity*: the insensitivity and manipulative style of the failed group, meant that they didn't manage to build up a network of cooperative, mutually beneficial relationships. The successful appreciated diversity and were able to cooperate with and get along with a range of different colleagues.

Compare the emotionally competent manager with the stereotypical gender characteristics and what do you find? The woman manager!

## Conclusions

There may or may not be a biological basis for these types of competencies or for aggressiveness and competitiveness – but on a daily basis women practise emotional competency far more frequently than do men. Women are also used to losing out a good proportion of the time – and it would be surprising, given the nature of the professions and senior management, if Superwoman had not had to suffer many career disappointments on her route to the top. Men who succeed have probably had fewer of those and so are more likely to flounder when things don't go their way. Women have had to learn from their mistakes. Now the crack in the glass ceiling is in reach, women no longer fear success in the way that Horner described. Women know that they don't have to lose their feminine identity to be successful. Definitions of femininity are broader than in the early 20th century. Being a woman today means that you can try to have it all – family, friends and career. You don't have to worry that your 'brains' will prevent you from becoming a wife, lover and mother. Femininity is more diverse than it has ever been before.

# It is still a man's world!

*Having it all at work*

*A career for a man is like motherhood for a woman. Anyone who admits not being completely enamoured with the role appropriate for his sex is committing blasphemy.*[1]

*There is no doubt that in many ways, women have made progress towards achieving equality in the workplace. However, real problems remain to be addressed, with women earning significantly less than their male colleagues for no reason other than their sex, with sexual harassment still endemic and with discrimination on the basis of sex unacceptably common.*[2]

*For too many women there is a glass ceiling over their aspirations – it allows them to see where they might be going but stops them getting there. In any given occupation and in any given public position, the higher the rank, prestige or power, the smaller the proportion of women.*[3]

A professional *career* is still seen by many as unsuitable
and unnatural for a woman, although women are now
accepted in professional *roles*. Thus while a female barris-
ter may be commonplace, her aspirations to become a
judge, may be perceived as socially undesirable. In
British universities for example, more than 25 years
since the introduction of equal pay legislation, the gap
between the pay of men and women remains firmly in
place. Women earn 18% less than men for the same
work at the same level. In the USA among academic
psychologists, men are more likely to hold a higher
faculty rank and are thus more likely to have tenure
than women. And universities are supposed to be *en-
lightened* institutions.

The world of work in general belongs firmly in the
hands of men and the more important or influential your
chosen career – the harder the men in charge will fight to
keep it that way. The boundaries of the battlefield though,
are often unclear. The fight may be one of stealth, deceit,
betrayal, abuse and violence. It may be one of gentle
persuasion, but it is a man's game. Women learn the
rules as they go along. There are no road maps to guide
you.

## Having it all – at work

We have been encouraged to believe that we can have it
all – and so we try. But there are still obstacles to achieving
the goal that are not always obvious, particularly to those
of us who are sceptical about feminism or the kinds of
explanations that make sex and gender important. There
is no escaping the fact that, despite women's achieve-

ments, we still fail consistently to gain the kind of power that today's Superwoman might legitimately seek.

While women have been entering the established professions in North America and north-western Europe in large numbers over the past 15 years, there are still very few who have reached the top. In 1990 in the UK, The Hansard Society, whose aims are to promote greater knowledge of and participation in democratic government, produced a report called 'Women on Top'. They concluded that:

> *There are still formidable barriers which stop women getting to the top: of structures, of working practices, of tradition and above all of attitudes. But there is strong evidence of what organisations can do to break down all of these barriers. It would take only a small amount of determination to make sure this country ceases to under-use nearly half of its talent. We urge Government and Parliament, industry and commerce, the professions, academia and the various branches of the public service to act on our recommendations, so that we may now cover at speed the last long mile of the journey towards equality. It can be done.*[4]

A similar pattern of barriers persists over 10 years later and is characteristic of Western industrial societies across the world. In the profession of medicine in 1999 less than one quarter of all top clinical posts were held by women, and in highly paid specialties such as surgery this fell to 5.4%. In UK universities in 1999 only 9.8% of full professors were women. Moreover, the more prestigious the institution, the *lower* the proportion of female professors – so when women do enter the higher ranks of professional life it appears that they have a far harder time breaking through barriers in high-status specialties and high-status institutions. The model persists throughout employment in the media, in industry, in the legal profession and in relation to influential public appointments.

Women clearly still have to be *outstanding* in order to occupy the same ranks and take up similar opportunities as those available to men. It is therefore no wonder that women drive themselves so hard – to try to become Super-women. One such example is Genevieve Berger, mother of two teenagers and herself a Superwoman, appointed recently to head up France's foremost body of scientific research, the National Centre for Scientific Research (CNRS). A media profile of the organisation and Berger describes them accordingly:

> *A few years ago France's foremost body of scientific research was criticised for being immobile, too narrowly specialised and bureaucratic.*
>
> *Wearing a chic trouser suit with golden jewellery, her blonde hair in a spiky style, Genevieve Berger, its director since September 2000, does not match this image. ... Berger is representative of the new order – young and innovative, with a multidisciplinary training.*[5]

That training, it turns out, involves her holding a triple doctorate in physical sciences, medicine and human biology and having had an award-studded career. And she is only in her mid-forties.

The fact that she heads an organisation in which there are 10,700 women employees to 14,600 men and the women hold the technical and administrative posts and the men the scientific ones is a disheartening surprise. Out of the 130 directors of research there are only five women, and Berger has set herself the task to improve the role of women in the CNRS. Berger is quoted as saying that the reasons for the disproportionate number of men to women in the key posts are complex:

> *It is to do with notions of power, and men and women have different systems of networks. Women have many other constraints and have to organise their time differently.*

There are several important points to be drawn from Berger's case. Firstly, judging by the qualifications described, she has had to work twice as hard as any male colleague to reach her current position of influence. Secondly, Berger herself makes the point that women have constraints on their lives that do not apply to men. These are not only the key constraints applied to women who have to run the home as well as their working lives, although these are difficult enough; they are also about the fact that women do not have the helpful and supportive networks of people in key positions that men have. This is at least in part because there are so few of us up there. Sadly, it seems that when women are successful it is far too often the case that they behave as Queen Bees to keep away their rivals. The idea of supporting the future careers of other women is anathema. The British Prime Minister throughout most of the 1980s, Margaret Thatcher, was a case in point. So many women, from all political points of view, rejoiced at the arrival of a woman in this position. However, she did little to help either women in politics or the lives of ordinary women in Britain.

Thirdly, we as women do not have many good role models with whom to identify, other than the numerous media images of Superwomen. Real women, with whom we could identify and from whom we could learn, are very rare. They are so rare that, of course, like Berger, we perceive them to be Superwomen also – so how do we manage to develop *suitable* aspirations if the only images we are confronted with are those of Nicole Kidman and Genevieve Berger?

## Real women's lives

> *I left school desperate to get married, so I'd done my 'A' levels and then run away from everyone's good advice and having got married and had my first child, I started doing an Open University degree which I got halfway through when my husband died and I had to go to work. I really didn't think any more of it until my kids started doing 'A' levels and I thought either I'm going to spend my next two years washing or we're all going to study together.*[6]

This extract from an interview study of psychology undergraduates in the UK shows up a difference between the classic trajectory of women's lives (i.e. falling in love, fairy-tale marriage and living happily ever after) and real life. For women who are now 40 years of age and older, it is likely that they expected to fulfil themselves primarily through motherhood and marriage and a satisfying career would be secondary. For many of us, the dream does not work out that way. Many women become single parents – frequently against their will – through widowhood or more commonly divorce. While their preference might be for domestic life, many find they get a great deal of satisfaction from work and a career that they never expected to have.

However, as we know, these combination lives are not the easy option – and most of us combine work and motherhood.

Over the years since 1990 the number of women in employment in the UK rose by more than 843,000, which is getting on for three times the rise in the number of men. In spring 2000 41% of working-age women in the UK in employment had dependent children, and more than two-thirds of women with dependent children now work outside the home. The pattern of mothers' employment is that 54% of those with preschool children are in employment, and this rises to 69% of those with primary school children and 75% of those with children aged 11–15; those with older children are almost all in work.[7]

Over the past 30 years, an increasing amount has been written about women's lives. It mostly focuses upon the conflicting requirements of home, family, partner and work and emphasises that most women do not have the opportunity to be in a relationship and have a family and a career without a significant price to pay – whether it is in their own health, in their relationships with their partners and children or in career success. These ideas go back almost 40 years to when Hannah Gavron and, later, Ann Oakley initially brought the home into the spotlight with their respective books, *The Captive Wife* and *Housewife*.[8] More recently, attention has been focused on the world of work and juggling home and career.[9] The message is the same though: women have complicated and potentially stressful lives and many try to have it all – and often with clear degrees of success – but eventually something has to give.

In the Internet Health Journal[10] a discussion of Sue Barton's research showed that ordinary professional women are under a great deal more stress than their male counterparts.

*The problem is that women feel as if they must do everything as if it is the only thing they are doing ... They take on ever-more responsibilities, then are reluctant to compromise or set new priorities with what they are already accomplishing. ... research indicates that for men, coming home from work usually means an end to the primary source of stress for the day. But for women, leaving work offers no refuge. If the house is a mess and food isn't on the table, many women feel it reflects on their abilities as an adequate wife or mother. And if marital relations are strained or kids aren't doing well, women tend to internalise these problems, feeling they are due to some failing or other.*

These pressures are real and different women find different ways of coping. However, it is clearly the case that women's real lives hold back their careers. Our lives are also detrimental to our health and to our sense of selfhood and identity.

## Conflicts at work: challenges to having it all

But it is not only the home/work conflicts that make life difficult for those who are trying to balance home and career. There is a great deal that goes on at work that serves to exhaust us, throw our lives into confusion and use up our reserves of emotional energy.

Do women have to become like men to succeed in their careers? Do we have to shed our sense of being a good mother and wife or partner? Do we have to work the ways that men seem to do if they wish to succeed? Some of today's Superwomen believe they have to work harder and better than men to get to the important top rungs of the ladder. What they don't know is that the obstacles to success are visible only if you have the means to see them. Choosing career success needs to be conducted carefully in the full awareness of the physical and emotional landscape that needs to be navigated.

## Beware of hazards

It is tempting to believe that it is only the women who fall by the wayside and *don't* reach giddy heights, who complain about sexism in the workplace or the pressure that domestic life places upon career prospects. That would be a mistake and any potential Superwoman who ignores the evidence that sexism at work is rife, is likely to come crashing down far harder than her more cynical sisters. Taking note of the barriers is not the same as throwing up your hands and giving in. But entering the world of high-status work is *entering the world of men* and to do that we need a map. We are not men and so it doesn't come naturally.

Sheila, who has retired now, was a lawyer in a prestigious firm. She gained entry to university at a time when relatively few women did so. She excelled in her work, achieving the best grades in her final year and was head-hunted along with the best men of her generation of law school graduates. She realised very soon that to succeed (or more correctly to survive) she needed to become very tough-minded. She had to deny some of the things she had earlier believed to be key principles. She had believed in cooperation and being part of a team. It was soon made clear to Sheila that each person had to show themselves to be 'the best'. This meant she could not leave room for sharing information, which she had made the mistake of doing previously and then finding her ideas and the fruits of her efforts being credited to colleagues who then gained favour.

Somehow she never found the time to marry, although she would have liked to have done. She did have relationships with men, including a long-standing affair with a married man. Her life revolved around work and she had few friends, not because she was unpopular but, as the years passed by, she had relatively little in common with other women. Even those who graduated with her gave up the law to have a family, or veered away from chasing the careers they once aspired to. Sheila realised one day that she was on her own, and was particularly distressed by the younger women entering her profession who openly despised her for being 'old-fashioned' and unmarried. It seemed to Sheila that what she had achieved at great personal cost, was seen by others to be for nothing, as she didn't have it all.

## Mapping the territory

To be successful in a career, we have to negotiate our way around the prevailing expectations that accompany the female sex – principally that motherhood and its associated responsibilities should be paramount. Women's careers, to fulfil their potential for success, have to be taken seriously, not only by the individual concerned, but by key people in the organisation. So what strategies have successful women developed to bypass prescriptions based on gender that consign the majority of women to junior levels in organisations?

Researchers in the UK have developed a profile of the woman who makes a success of her career.[11] Is this a further clue to the character of Superwoman?

- she is likely to be first-born in her family
- she is likely to have had supportive parents who encouraged self-assertion and independence
- she is well-educated
- she comes from an educated and financially well-off family
- her personality includes a strong belief in her own abilities
- while she acknowledges her luck to a small extent, she really attributes her success to her efforts and hard work
- she is more innovative than the majority of other women
- she has a high need for achievement

As the researchers themselves say of these successful women:

> *Many of our successful women mentioned the importance of persistence and stressed the need to 'keep battling' to achieve their objectives. They felt that success required making an extra effort and that the process of achieving success is harder for a woman to achieve, they also stressed that women should not allow their femininity to become an issue. Women were discouraged from having a 'chip on their shoulder' ... In addition, a number of our successful women emphasised the need to let those in power know their ambitions.[12]*

Career-directed Superwomen don't want to acknowledge
that their gender might have a negative effect on their
ambitions. They see themselves as achieving on their
merits and fear that any gesture towards feminism
would indicate a 'chip on the shoulder', which would be
a serious mistake.

## Barriers to success and the downfall of a Queen Bee

Cissy thought she was able to make a success of her career
on her own merits and remain 'feminine'. She was a
natural politician, in that she had an instinct for where
power lay at any one time in the organisations she
worked in, and she quickly found a way of aligning
herself with those people and making herself indispens-
able. She moved from a junior college to an established
university. She worked nearby and there was a post to
help establish an entry programme for mature students
from disadvantaged groups in line with government
policy. She landed the job because she had far more
knowledge of these potential students than anyone in the
Ivory Tower. Cissy arrived at work each day in stunning
clothes and some of the other women noted that earrings
and eye make-up matched each new outfit. One colleague
declared, 'I don't think the male professors have any idea
how long it takes to present yourself like that each day!'.
   What was important though was that it became very
clear to the women (and some of the men) who worked
alongside her that she did not deliver on the access to
students. However, the senior professor in the department
publicly blamed the academic staff for not meeting the

targets. In the meantime Cissy climbed the department hierarchy and was the one and only woman to take an executive role. At first the academic staff were pleased – but why was the previously affable senior professor always coming down on their heads about their lack of attention to unqualified student access? Why were they being told that they had not attended meetings that he believed they should be at but of which they had had no knowledge? Was Cissy feeding this information to him? Surely not – she often talked about her liberal politics and her role on women's committees, even though she stopped short of calling herself a feminist. But she gradually made more mistakes – and one day a woman colleague was quite disturbed to find Cissy in a rage muttering about a colleague who only had to flutter her eyes to get what she wanted. Shortly after that Cissy was involved with one or two other very senior university staff in going around the university and then the local area providing strategy talks. She began hers with a giggle saying she wasn't very good at technology and she proceeded to have problems with her Power-point presentation. Cissy shortly afterwards left for another high-profile job with a man who had been her boss at the junior college. Despite her high salary, her increasingly high profile in the university and her freedom to carve out the post in the way she wanted, Cissy could not sustain herself in the organisation. She believed she could behave like a Queen Bee (the *only* high-profile, powerful woman) while paying lip-service to being a supporter of equal opportunities and women's rights. She also got caught up in not knowing how to be feminine *and* powerful, and in her idea that femininity was about being exploitative and using it to influence senior men. She alternated between the roles of being strong and supportive and being just a helpless woman. That might have worked, and indeed did work for a while; but she then fell into the trap of turning against other women

| Internal barriers | External barriers |
|---|---|

**Internal barriers**

- Lack of self-confidence
- Home does not provide a refuge
- Adopting stereotypical female role
- Confused sense of how to be feminine and powerful
- Not recognising gender issues
- Becoming bitter and aggressive

**External barriers**

- Exclusion from the 'old boys' network'
- Lack of mentors and female role models
- Lack of peer support/ isolation
- Attitudes of other women (e.g. secretaries and junior colleagues)
- Sexist remarks and sexual harassment
- Institutionalised sexism and unconcious sexism in senior colleagues

**Figure 7**  Barriers to Superwoman's career success.

and accusing them of what she herself probably feared she was doing – using her femininity to get where she wanted to, rather than her skills. She was aware that gender was a major organisational issue and a barrier to career progress, but she was not aware of the extent to which gender is a trap for *all* women. Women have to work twice as hard as men. They cannot afford to play political games unless they have the professional track record and the networks. That rule *always* applies to women. It applies to men much of the time.

But whatever today's Superwoman believes about her success being consequent on abilities and efforts, the overwhelming evidence from psychologists and other social scientists is that barriers exist in work organisations as well as in individual women themselves. What is more, the internal and external barriers are not easily separated.

## Overcoming internal barriers

Cissy's experience provided examples of a range of barriers to women's career success – internal and external.

## Self-confidence

Cissy entered a university in her early forties, with a career in junior college education and management behind her, but she was in an anomalous position. Other senior university staff had moved up through the academic or administrative ranks. Academics who were not in senior management roles were still autonomous professionals who would need a great deal of convincing that a non-academic manager had something to offer them before they would fall into line. Cissy had the confidence to go for the job – but she was astute enough to realise very quickly that she was in a cleft stick and needed to find a means of ensuring she could be effective. She lacked the confidence to be honest about her aims and abilities and thus neither she nor any of her colleagues knew what to make of her role. This had the effect of reducing her self-confidence.

- Think about your 'self' – what are your psychological type preferences? Are you going against type in your day-to-day role, the job you do or the way you do it?
- Confidence comes through recognising your weaknesses *and* strengths, admitting them to yourself and to your colleagues, and deciding what to do about it.
- You don't have to be good at everything.
- If you find you are in the wrong job – have the confidence to look for another!

## Home does not provide a refuge

This was not a problem for Cissy whose children were adults and whose husband was very supportive; but it is a clear problem for many Superwomen. For instance:

*It's another Friday evening and I find myself exhausted, both physically and emotionally. I just pulled into the driveway after a half-hour battle with rush hour traffic, road-raged drivers, and heavy fog. Prior to the drive, I spent eight hours dealing with corporate politics, co-worker antics, and self-reminders that my annual pay increase isn't coming for another ten months. I'm tired. I fall into the sofa and allow myself a moment of serenity.*

*But no more than 60 seconds later, I find myself scurrying around the kitchen washing the coffee pot, disinfecting the countertop, and straightening up the mail. After conquering the kitchen, I find myself drawn to the living room where I proceed to sort out the stacks of magazines that have been accumulating since what seems like the last presidential election. And in my mind I'm trying to plan a perfect evening for my husband and three sons packed with dinner, a movie and a stop at the arcade.*

*At the time I didn't think much about my compulsion to seek out more tasks and activities to pursue despite my obvious need for rest and relaxation. Only later, as I began writing the outline for this very article did it enter my consciousness that I too, suffer from Superwoman Syndrome.*[13]

Women are in danger of losing or annihilating themselves in order to achieve the impossible. The important issue is to be true to yourself. That, like the woman quoted above, might involve re-ordering your priorities and reassessing your life. Her decision was to change her domestic priorities.

> *[She] ... let the cleaning wait a day, enjoyed
> dinner out with my family, and then let my
> husband escort the kids to the arcade as I went
> home early to take a candle-lit bath. To my sur-
> prise it actually felt good (not guilt-ridden) to
> make these adjustments. ... The result? A fresh,
> bushy-tailed woman on Saturday morning who is
> relaxed and happy about spending the day with
> her husband and three children.*

This woman clearly focused on *doing it all* as well as trying
to have it all. Her solution was to assert her own needs and
share the load at home. She appeared to have succeeded in
making her home a refuge rather than the site of additional
chores and stress.

## Adopting the stereotypical female role

Cissy chose to do the 'helpless female' alongside the
'power-dressed Queen Bee' and the occasional 'protector
of women's rights'.

Cary Cooper and Marilyn Davidson[14] have identified
a range of roles that women managers play, but find each
of them to be a potential source of executive stress.
Cooper and Davidson suggest that because there are so
few women in senior positions, those who are there take
on roles that they believe *others perceive* to be conducive to
a senior woman manager. Successful women have to 're-
invent' themselves in some way which can cause them
stress and anxiety if their adopted role and view of themselves is incompatible with others' definition of the role.
The difficulty for women is specifically when there is
conflict in relationship C, i.e. when Superwoman's perception of others' definition of the executive role is at
variance with her own. The usual characteristics of that

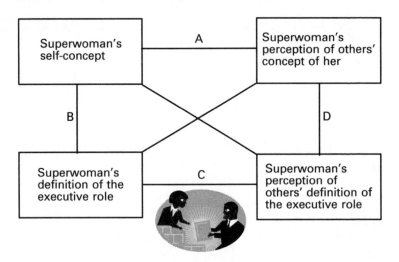

**Figure 8**   Role expectations and stress (adapted from Cooper and Davidson[14]).

role relate closely to *what men are like* rather than to what women are like. Superwoman, because of her sex, is unlikely to be seen as fitting that role at first glance. Complications also arise in the D relationship – her perception of herself in relation to how she perceives that others see her role. The roles that women invent for themselves in order to overcome some of these difficulties bring problems of their own, but they also enable others to see them as fitting in to the organisational structure. Each role has benefits and pitfalls. Some can be usefully adapted$^{\$\$\$}$ and others are to be avoided at all costs$^{!!!}$:

TOKEN WOMAN OR QUEEN BEE$^{\$\$\$}$

This has some benefits at first because it appears to be powerful and high-profile. But, like Cissy, it can leave Superwoman stranded and isolated if she does not find a support network that she can trust.

### MOTHER EARTH[$$$]

This is a common role that Superwomen try to adopt, and involves being the confessor or counsellor, or taking on motherly roles towards other senior and mid-level colleagues. It is time-consuming and bolsters an image of passive or nurturant femininity, rather than one which exudes professional effectiveness. However, it does frequently provide a woman with information, and sometimes loyalty, that might not be available to male colleagues. It has the advantage of enabling Superwoman to be seen as feminine while taking on a senior position. The important thing is to ensure that you don't use up all your energy in this role, and that you do it 'naturally' rather than against type.

### THE PET ROLE[!!!]

Becoming a pet or a mascot means that stress may be reduced in some ways, but it is a sure way of remaining on the side lines and not being included in top-level decision-making. While Superwoman may gain some attention through being amusing, looking very attractive or whatever she does to maintain this position, ultimately, self-confidence will be eroded because her intellect and competencies will not be taken seriously if she is the executive mascot.

### THE SEDUCTRESS ROLE[!!!]

In this role Superwoman is viewed, first and foremost, as sexually attractive to her male colleagues, and this detracts from her credibility. Superwoman has to maintain a balance between paying attention to her clothes, which must be smart and attractive, and maintaining her femininity while not being flirtatious or seductive.

## DEVIANT, MAN-HATER AND FEMINIST!!! $$$

This role is paradoxical to say the least. In order to become Superwomen we have to work hard, try not to be seductive, maintain our femininity, avoid being sexually harassed or discriminated against, form networks with other women if we can, take ourselves and our competencies seriously, and be fully aware that gender is an issue and yet we also need to avoid being seen as 'feminist' which carries the connotations of 'deviant' and 'man-hater'.

## Overcoming external barriers

> *Blatant sex discrimination includes those discriminatory actions directed against women that are quite obvious to most observers and are highly visible.*[15]

External barriers fall into two categories – the ones that are *easily visible*, such as the lack of female role models and mentors and the attitudes of other women, and the *invisible ones*, such as unconscious sexism and institutionalised sexism. Barriers to Superwoman's success such as sexual harassment or lack of equal pay or equal opportunities policies are best dealt with formally in cooperation with the organisation.

Charlotte, for example, having read the company's strategic plan for investing in equal opportunity and non-discriminatory policies, volunteered to work with the human resources department to survey attitudes and expectations of women and minority staff and set up a strategic task-force. The fact that she was a woman in a relatively senior role, and thus had credibility from her juniors and from the top managers, meant that her initiative both was welcome and proved to be effective, as she received cooperation from all levels of the company.

Pippa was in a different position though. She was very fond of her immediate boss, and he was prepared to back her in many innovative projects. However, when it came to key decision-making committees and representing the organisation elsewhere she was always overlooked. When she confronted him, he was surprised and said that, although he considered her a valued colleague and good friend, he often felt her ideas and aspects of her behaviour were at odds with corporate policy. He described her as 'a bit of a loose cannon'. She was stunned as she believed that the organisation valued the originality of her contribution. It seemed to Pippa, and to her women friends, that James, her boss, could only see her as different and thus somehow out of place because she was a *confident and competent woman*. She was indeed different from many of the other women who worked there in junior positions, as they were far less assertive. She was also different from her male colleagues who conformed to the boss's view of organisational life.

So why is it that so many senior male colleagues can only see you as a woman and not as a colleague? There is no simple answer to this question nor is there a simple solution. The reason that women are seen as *women* is because of the deeply held views about gender differences that have become so much part of all cultures. They are difficult to escape. The solution, in part, relies on awareness of the issues. Both women and men should take on the responsibility for challenging discrimination – because it is vital that the best staff are employed appropriately. However, as many men *still* seem unable to grasp the fact that their colleagues and clones are not always the best people, the onus falls upon women to shift the status quo. We need to understand the way women are seen in workplace organisations and this means facing up to some unpalatable truths that feminists have been identifying for several years. Women are frequently seen for their sexual potential – and women themselves frequently accept this.

## Sex, harassment and exploitation

The sexual exploitation of women by men occurs when men have direct power over women's conditions of work, their hiring and firing, as in the case of secretaries, shop-floor factory workers, waitresses and domestic staff. These workers tend to have little power, in that their lack of formal qualifications and skill makes them easily replaceable. As one academic describes it:

> *In such jobs a woman is employed as a woman. She is also, apparently, treated like a woman, with one aspect of this being specifically sexual. Specifically, if part of the reason a woman is hired is to be pleasing to the male boss, whose notion of a qualified worker merges with a sexist notion of the proper role of women, it is hardly surprising that sexual intimacy, forced when necessary, would be considered part of her duties and his privileges.*[16]

However, it is not only 'blue collar' men who enjoy these luxuries. As Naomi Wolf[17] observes, the rules which governed employment in what had been specifically 'display professions', such as fashion modelling, acting, night club

hostessing and so on, where beauty had been a requirement, appear to have been extended.

> *What is happening today is that all the professions
> into which women are making strides are being
> rapidly reclassified – so far as the women are con-
> cerned – as display professions.*

Thus female bank managers, lawyers and headteachers of
schools all have to look both powerful and sexy. The
appearance of Marcia Clark, the female prosecution
lawyer in the O. J. Simpson murder trial, which was tele-
vised throughout the world, has been the subject of direct
discussion. Television programmes, news and comment
in the media focused on the length of her skirts and
manner of clothing. This reached a crescendo when she
changed her hairstyle. Why should this be the case? Her
legal skills, clearly on display, were deemed by the media
to be less relevant to the proceedings than her sexual
appeal. Her colleagues and the defence lawyers (mostly
men) were discussed in a variety of ways, but it was only
with *her*, that appearance was on the agenda. Women as
professionals have to tread a tightrope between visibility
and invisibility *because of this positioning as sexual*; and
dress style, gestures and language are part of this.

Some occupations for women are seen as almost
equivalent to mistress/sex object. Secretaries, waitresses,
sales staff and nurses in particular, have traditionally been
seen in this way by the men who work in a superordinate
rank. An example of one secretarial college attempting
to help their graduates ensure employment included the
advice to 'sell' themselves by becoming a 'Pretty
package'.[18]

One of the most blatant contexts for women being seen
as sex objects by men, while they are seeing themselves as

potential professionals, is the university. There, some male academics appear to judge all female students by appearance, and see them as potential sexual partners, regardless of whether they themselves or the students are married or with partners. Indeed, the practice of married lecturers having serial sexual encounters with female students is so embedded in the cultural mores of academic life that it could almost be positioned as a 'privilege' of the occupation (see, for instance, Malcolm Bradbury's *The History Man*).

In my book, *Gender, Power and Organisation*, I quote the following example, reported by feminist academic researchers, of an encounter by a group of male and female academics in a psychology department in the UK:

*(At interview)*

**female staff:** *Are you ready to interview another prospective student yet?*

**male colleague:** *Yes. What have you got there? I don't want just anyone – give me another of those pretty little girls.*

**female staff:** *Have you got the rest of the application forms there?*

**male colleague:** *You don't need to see them. All we need to know is if they've got long blonde hair and big boobs.*

*(At assessment)*

**female staff:** *I'm not sure which student hasn't handed in her essays yet.*

**male colleague:** *You must know. Brown hair. So ugly you wouldn't even want to mug her.*[19]

Male North American university academics appear to have similar expectations about the *raison d'être* of female students. This often comes as a shock to the young women involved. One study revealed that 26% of male academics admitted to sexual involvement with female students.[20] One woman academic reported the following:

> *My whole feeling about surviving in a large university was to get to know my faculty members, so that when they were grading the papers, they were dealing with a person. So I'd always try to meet the people who were teaching my courses. When I went about doing that, one of my professors made an appointment for me to come to his office in the evening. I didn't think anything was weird about it. It wasn't convenient, but everybody had busy schedules. But when I got down there, it was quite clear that he has something else in mind. And it was very hard to figure out how to react. He kissed me, and I didn't know what to do at first. I got slightly involved, and then I thought, wait a minute: this is really weird. And I found a way to get out of the office and back to my dormitory. Clearly if I'd been willing, we'd have had sex right there on the floor of his office.*[21]

This woman, ambitious and serious about her university education and future career, was seen by the lecturer in the framework of *his* needs as offering herself sexually. He was incapable it seemed of treating a woman as a peer or potential peer, only as a sex object.

How far are members of organisations aware of the implications of their own behaviour? The young female

professional or manager attending the board meeting for
the first time only experiences her own strangeness and
terror with the situation. She is noticeable, in the minority
as a woman; the men know each other and are like each
other; men are familiar with the routine and assist new-
comers. How can she know why some board members fear
her presence? She sees herself as new and inexperienced.
Some of them know from her qualifications and background that she is on the 'fast track'. They may feel
unable to welcome her as she represents a threat. Thus
they behave as if she is invisible and a burden. But why is
she perceived as such a threat? There is no evidence that
women are going to take over companies or professional
groups in any large numbers.

The male head of a division finds it difficult to cope
when he knows that the new female recruit is better qual-
ified for *his* job than he is himself. As time passes she
wonders what more on earth she has to do to get his
attention and praise. He is terrified that his incompeten-
cies will be exposed and does what he (legitimately) can to
hinder her finding them out, and thus obstructs her
progress.

## Conclusions

As women we need to pay attention to the messages of
feminist scholars. They are the result of years of research
into gender relations in organisations and, however much
we like men, and however much we like particular men,
there are man-made barriers to career achievement that
need to be understood before they can be overcome. As
Dorothy Smith asserts:

*Men attend to and treat as significant only what men say. The circle of men whose writing and talk was significant to each other extends backwards in time as far as our records reach. What men were doing was relevant to men, was written by men about men for men. Men listened and listen to what one another said.*[22]

Widespread discrimination still occurs throughout organisations and this has consequences for all women and men. Women who break through the traditional career barriers, shattering the glass ceiling, are no less subject to the processes than those who do not.

# Motherhood versus the glittering career

*Coping with the backlash*

*The question of motherhood versus career seems, for the majority, to have been stably resolved in the direction of combining them. They seem to have made a unanimous and unconflicted choice to experience occupational involvement, marriage and motherhood.*[1]

*Liz wiped the cereal out of Daisy's hair and, fending off the sticky hands that lunged for her suit, kissed the tender nape of her neck. Reluctantly she handed her over to Susie, the nanny, and tried to persuade Jamie to let go of her leg so that she could check her briefcase. As usual he wailed and clung like a limpet.*[2]

*Becoming* a mother is something that most women can do, and *only* women can do. While increasingly women recognise that they have the choice to opt out of motherhood, it is still the case that nine out of ten of us have at least one child. So most of us take the fact of motherhood or future motherhood for granted. *Being* a mother, though, is increasingly a *lifestyle choice* for women. Do I stay at home and engage in full-time child care? Do I have children in my early twenties or late thirties? Do I have them with or without a partner? Do I combine motherhood and a career and remain Superwoman?

## Lifestyle choices for Superwoman

What kind of lifestyle are we talking about when we include motherhood in the equation? Academic study after study has shown the following patterns of motherhood to be true:

- Most women opt to become mothers if they can.
- Increasing numbers of these mothers work outside the home.
- Most women combine work/career and motherhood. For some it is purely for economic reasons, but for a significant and increasing minority of working mothers it is so they continue a successful career.
- Women who are the most successful tend to have fewer children. In academia in the UK for example, where promotion to full professor is only likely to happen to one in 30 women, those who are promoted are more likely to have no children or only one child.
- Women in all professional jobs mostly put off motherhood until their late thirties.
- Despite the rhetoric about the 'new man' and men wanting to take a fully active part in parenting, the

basic *management* of the home, child carers and child care tasks still fall *mainly* to women.

- If the man opts for the primary parent role, the family is likely to be less well-off financially, because women are almost always paid around 25% less than their male counterpart in any job.

- A woman who would normally want to have a stimulating job or an active career is unlikely to be happy for very long if she opts for a long career-break or leaves work altogether for full-time motherhood.

- Children who are cared for by a reluctant or depressed person are less likely to be well-adjusted socially or to develop intellectually as well as children who have more than one regular carer. Thus two parents, or sharing child care with a good, regular nanny is the best approach to infant/young child care.

- Mothers are made to feel guilty for almost every possible problem their child might have at present or in their future lives, and most mothers accept this guilt as their own!

- It is almost impossible to consider yourself a good mother.

- All mothers feel guilty – whatever kind of lifestyle they have – at least some of the time.

Most Superwomen become *Superwomen at work* before they add motherhood and all that that entails, to their list of accomplishments. The reasons for glittering careers preceding motherhood are probably obvious, but worth repeating all the same.

1   Looking after children is *demanding and exhausting*.

2   Motherhood on a full-time basis has the effect of

making women *feel inadequate* and reluctant even to consider tackling the corporate world.

**3**  It is difficult to consider your options and *develop your career strategy* when you are bogged down in child-centred activities, however much you might enjoy them and however rewarding they undoubtedly are.

**4**  Many organisations expect 'high-flyers' to identify themselves at an early stage. If you become a mother at the time that high-flying men and women without children are getting onto the corporate or career ladder, you will miss that early boat. That means, instead of getting ahead along with your peers, you might be in danger of entering the growth stage in your career along with younger, more energetic people who promise to be high-flyers. Thus you are in danger of being overlooked.

**5**  If you are young when you have your children, you will be *relatively poor* compared to parents already established in their careers. The less you can afford, the less flexible your child care arrangements are likely to be.

## Expectations versus reality: what do you do when the baby arrives?

*Whatever happened to ambitions to travel/write novels/change world, etc.? Too tired to care.*[3]

Superwoman may not have given the motherhood lifestyle a great deal of thought until she starts her maternity leave. That is when your thoughts turn in earnest to thinking about what you have let yourself in for! They usually go something like this:

1   Help! I am about to become a mother – we need to decorate the nursery and buy the cot, pram and baby clothes. If all goes well, that is fun.

2   What will the baby be like, will I be a good mother, what am I most likely to find difficult?

Almost everyone gets the second thought wrong! People ignore the one major issue – lack of sleep. You think because you have managed on 4 hours a night when you are travelling around on business or trying to get reports finished to a deadline, that you will manage night feeds. But somehow it isn't like that – looking after a baby in the night, changing it, feeding it, comforting it and caring for it – takes *emotional* energy. The stresses and strains that kept you up late at night for your work were different.

1   When you were on business trips and working to deadlines you could count on your other needs being looked after by someone else. In times when this wasn't the case, you had the time to look after yourself. *When you are awake at night with your baby, that sleep deprivation comes on top of a day (or more likely several days) when you have hardly been able to find the time to brush your teeth!*

2   When you had little sleep in order to accomplish those work-related tasks, you were doing something

at which you were very experienced and often the acknowledged expert. That didn't mean that it was easy – but you knew when you had got it right. *When you are awake at night comforting a crying baby, you are not the expert. You have only had a few weeks at being a mother and you don't know whether you have fed him too much, or too little, whether you have managed to wind him or whether he is in pain for some reason.*

**3** When you are dealing with problems at work you can call upon your own and others' experiences – problem-solving is a team effort. Once the solution is found you can rest, take leave or go out and celebrate on the way home from work. *When you have a worry about your baby and why she cannot sleep, you are emotionally involved and anxious, and although you and your partner both work out the solutions, you both feel isolated and the reward is managing to get some relief and a little more sleep.*

**4** If you succeed at work – win a contract, win a particular case, get promoted, get a paper published you become recognised for what you are – Superwoman. *The rewards of parenting are not immediate. For some they take a long time to arrive, and they are clouded by guilt and uncertainty. Infants don't have direct ways of saying 'thank you – you are Supermum'.*

What do women expect? Surely that is common sense? Well it doesn't look that way when you read about women's expectations. In a recent issue of a UK magazine directed towards pregnant women and new mothers,[4] three first-time pregnant women – Rosanna (aged 22) an

IT recruitment consultant, Catherine (aged 27) a teacher and Hilary (aged 38) a marketing and public relations director – were all asked what they were dreading and what they thought was in their medium-term futures. Rosanna dreaded 'weaning my baby on to solids – all that mess and food everywhere! ... I want to give my baby wholesome foods, but I'm not looking forward to the effort.' Catherine was concerned that she wouldn't be able to breastfeed – but 'I'm not worried about it though, I'm looking forward to it'. Hilary's '... biggest fear is not being able to meet my baby's needs if he's colicky or unhappy. I wonder if I'll be able to make sure he isn't upset.' Hilary's expectations summed up the Superwoman fallacy/fantasy:

*I'm planning to have six months off work before deciding whether to go back. Dino (her partner) says the baby will be a good excuse to finish work early and get home to spend time with us. I live in a part of London with a lot of people who don't work in offices, so I don't think I'll feel isolated because I'm not going out to work every day. I can't wait to go to messy play groups and mums and tots. I'll have less time to myself, but I hope I'll be able to get the odd leg wax and a trip to the gym in. Our gym has crèche facilities so there's no excuse!*

But there often is an excuse – exhaustion – and so much to do there is no time to have to yourself! The women were interviewed again after their babies had arrived. This is what Hilary said when her baby was 6 months old:

*It staggered me how much I loved her. I wasn't prepared for that intensity of feeling, or for the worry either!*

> *Tiredness is the most difficult thing. When Sophia was three and a half months old I became depressed. The tiredness was beginning to set in and I got low. ... I was dreading meeting Sophia's needs, but I'm actually very attentive. ... I try to make sure I'm reasonably presentable but I'm not as glamorous as I once was.*
>
> *... I was career oriented before having Sophia, but that's changed. I've amazed myself by deciding not to go back to work. ... I'd like to go back to my roots and do some fine art again. ... I can hardly believe how things have changed.[5]*

So Hilary chose to leave her career behind (at least for the time being). Rosanna confessed that:

> *Having Scarlet made me realise how shallow my job was. But I would be a liar if I said I don't envy former colleagues who've all since won promotions and bigger wage packets. I'm still hoping to do a massage course. I'm interested in holistic therapies and I think it's a profession I can fit around Scarlet. I couldn't leave her with a childminder or in a nursery – I'd be far too critical.[6]*

The magazine these women's experiences were described in, focused on motherhood as the primary concern, so it is no surprise that the women, however high-powered, would change their lives and put more emphasis on motherhood than career. The fact that *becoming a mother changes all women* was something that became very clear in my own research as well. Even the most dedicated career women among my respondents felt they had changed. They had more in common with other women, they felt more sympathy and concern for mothers, they thought about all children in ways they had not done previously. They all saw motherhood as *making a major contribution to the balance of their lives*, irrespective of how they chose to juggle between home and career.

In Maeve Haran's novel[7] about a 1990s Superwoman, Liz's (the heroine's) dilemmas are described. She is a high-profile, newly promoted TV programme controller, with a primary school age son and a preschool age daughter, a high-powered husband, a group of three close friends and a loyal nanny. In the extract below, she is talking to a hostile journalist:

*This was the fifth interview she'd given today, all of them trotting out the party line. Being a mother Wasn't a Problem; indeed it added to her Understanding of Everyday Concerns. Except that it was a problem. She never saw her children. Or her husband for that matter.*

*Maybe it was time to tell the truth. That women had been sold a pup. Having It All was a myth, a con, a dangerous lie. Of course you could have a career and a family. But there was one little frail detail the gurus of feminism forgot to mention: the cost to you if you did.*

*... Slowly she walked downstairs and sat opposite Steffi, refilling her glass and pouring another for herself. She was going to need it.*

*'You accused me of being consumed by guilt just now and I was about to deny it.' She took a sip. The wine and the relief of finally admitting to herself the price she was paying for her success were making her light-headed. 'But you're right, of course. The truth is I'm riddled with it.'[8]*

What is the answer to the dilemma though? For Liz it meant relationship and professional problems – although in the end, it all came together because her employers recognised that she had integrity and commitment. She was also (eventually!) seen in a good light because she didn't pretend she could do it all without stresses and strains! Her employers recognised that being honest with yourself and being aware of your limitations also meant a realistic approach to what can be done for the company – *a salutary and important message for every Superwoman.*

## You can still find a pathway to success!

For the super-talented Superwoman, your staying power, flexibility and resilience will always stand you in good stead, provided you know you can't always get *exactly* what you want and when you want it. *You need to know yourself.*

Consider the cases of Bobbie and Kate. Bobbie was 37 when she had her son Azriel. She had gone straight to university after high-school, gained a degree in law and, following her professional training, became a successful company lawyer and then moved up the hierarchy and took over the management of the firm's Far Eastern accounts. This meant that, while her office base remained in Sydney, Australia, she spent almost all of her working life in Japan, Malaysia, Hong Kong, Singapore and New York – that's when she wasn't in London! Her partner had a similar lifestyle, but like many couples they had always assumed that they would have children 'one day' and that day came soon after the death of her mother – it brought Bobbie down to earth for a while and made her feel the need for continuity and emotional fulfilment. Azriel arrived – a fine, healthy and beautiful son, and after 4 months at home, as planned, she felt more than ready to return to work, although she did feel reluctant to travel and leave him behind. So she re-negotiated her contract, and returned to her old speciality as a company lawyer. The hours were long, work had to be brought home as before, and accuracy and skill were demanded as routine. All of the workplace requirements were well within her capacity intellectually, emotionally and in terms of her stamina. However, Azriel became ill – he had a congenital heart condition that had not been picked up by the paediatrician earlier, and so was unexpected. However, it was not an unusual problem, and after 18 months of intermittent hospital treatment he was back to his normal good state of health. But that 18 months caused a great deal of distress for Bobbie. She could not always be relied on at work, she had to take days off, was initially called home by the nanny on several embarrassing occasions before Azriel's condition was diagnosed. Superwoman was under severe strain and she was not sure at first how to cope. She had been so used to hard work being the means to shining success. However, her achievements had stood her in good stead and she took time off work until her son's health had been returned to normal.

Kate went to university a couple of years after leaving school because she wanted to see more of the world beyond her middle-class Washington suburb. This was unusual for someone from her background. She had an excellent school record but considered herself a 'rebel' and eschewed the idea that she should take up a profession like her peers. Most of her contemporaries on the other hand were well aware of the need to gain certain career success steps by the time they reached the age of 30. After university, where she studied economics, Kate met and married a musician she had met in London and moved

over there to live. Soon they had two babies. They
thought they could live happily ever after, and in some
respects they did, except that Kate had always had Superwoman tendencies – she was intelligent, creative and un-
conventional – but soon realised that loving her partner
and children passionately was about *their* needs not hers.
She found herself short of time, short of energy and for
the first time in her life, lacking in confidence. Realising
this was, for Kate, the first rung of the ladder to her
glittering career: she completed a part-time doctorate,
began working in a university and became a full professor
at the age of 49, by which time she had published several
books and had been an economic consultant and adviser to
several governments throughout the word. The early days
of her career were slow and she recognised that, as the
children became more independent, her academic
output increased proportionately. Looking back she believed that she had had advantages over many of her
female colleagues and friends who had put off motherhood – she was *young* when her children were leaving
home. She saw her friends and colleagues becoming
tired and preoccupied with their families just as she
herself was gaining the momentum to go for the glittering
prizes.

Bobbie, Kate and almost all the other Superwomen I
know would not give up their careers or motherhood –
although many might have chosen to have done it differently. If only they had known!

# The emancipation of mothers:
# an oxymoron!

Superwomen of the generation that grew up to the expectation of having it all – motherhood and the glittering

career – were lucky in that they did have the choices that their mothers and older sisters did not. However, they lacked the experience and information that enabled them to be prepared – for the hard work, overwhelming emotional struggles, the tiredness, the strain and the guilt. They also lacked knowledge of the alternatives, good and bad, and of how to make *strategic choices* and *personal choices*. Today's Superwoman did not recognise that there were *different ways to have it all*.

Women above the age of 40 had had some experience or knowledge of struggles for the emancipation of women *from home*, at work. That generation, my generation, were brought up to witness the frustration of their mothers and grandmothers, and the low esteem in which women who were 'only mothers' were held. Women of high intellectual strength and integrity, often with a good education, were prevented from entering or re-entering the job market on marriage and almost certainly on becoming mothers. Many women only went to work in order to find a suitable husband. Their occupations were chosen with that goal in mind and thus secretarial and nursing jobs were particularly popular with middle-class women who wanted to marry the boss or a doctor. Then they would become mothers and stop work outside the home. It is interesting to see how in the 21st century, many jobs of that kind are now difficult to fill and the applicants tend to be from a lower social class background than they were 30 years ago. These days bosses marry bosses and doctors marry doctors, and it is unlikely that Superwomen chose their career paths by the type of man they might find there. This is not to say that Superwomen are not keen to find compatible partners and be happy in their relationships. It is that the requirement for a relationship for women and (many) men in the 21st century is for a marriage/partnership of equals. If you want to continue to be Superwoman, you certainly need to be with a partner who can appreciate the stresses and can support you. My generation, now in their fifties, also lived and worked with the other group of women who were derided, the 'unmarried career woman'. These were women who, before the birth of Superwoman, 'only' had their careers. They were vilified for 'giving up' the chance of a family and feminine fulfilment to live what was portrayed as a sterile, fruitless existence in pursuit of professional success. We were brought up to pity them and to see them for what they *lacked* rather than for the amazing contribution that many of these women made to their professions and the communities in which they lived. They were also further divided into those who had intended to marry, whose partners had been killed in the war, and those who had never intended to be wives and mothers. The latter were the worst kind – the unfeminine, the ungrateful – and represented a lifestyle to be avoided at all costs. At least the sacrifices made by the full-time mothers, who could have had a career, were applauded. To sacrifice the chance of motherhood was insupportable.

What made the difference to our understanding of how to make choices, was the way that feminist scholars, journalists and others were prepared to speak out, and described and challenged the impact of the patriarchal, or male-dominated, society for constraining the lives and talents of women. As Adrienne Rich, the frequently quoted feminist writer on motherhood, said:

> The 'childless woman' and the 'mother' are a false polarity which has served the institutions of both motherhood and heterosexuality ... We are, none of us, 'either' mothers or daughters; to our amazement, confusions, and greater complexity, we are both.[9]

In other words, she pointed out that we are women, and share with all other women, the dilemmas of having to make choices, and having to learn how to have it all without losing ourselves in the process. We don't have to marry. We don't have to be mothers. We don't have to have a career. We don't have to have relationships with our mothers, children or partners. However, it is possible to do all those things, and to do them in ways that enable survival. But those choices would not be possible were they not informed by the struggles and mistakes our mothers and their mothers made. The legacy of feminism, whether we like it or not, has enabled the rise of Superwoman. We need to ensure that we don't throw that away.

## The role of fathers in the lifestyle choice

**Did you know?** Two out of every three dads would like to stay at home and look after their babies while mum goes to work?[10]

Being female helps with mothering, but it is not enough. The biological family of mother and child is vulnerable; it needs protection and support. Mothers need sustenance, physical, mental and spiritual. In western society the person who is expected to provide the sustenance is the mother's husband, or partner, but only if he chooses.[11]

By the time she got downstairs, Daisy under one arm and the report she was supposed to have read in bed last night under the other, David was already immersed in the newspapers. As usual he let the chaos of the breakfast table lap around *him, getting his own toast but never offering to get anyone else's.*[12]

What about fathers? We certainly hear a great deal about them, and it is clear that children benefit from having good, lasting and quality relationships with both their parents. Despite the plaudits for men in their role as fathers, and claims that men would rather be in full-time child care than work, neither the research nor the anecdotal evidence supports this as a reality. We need to understand the difference between rhetoric and certainty in order to make the best decisions about how we manage parenting responsibilities.

Research shows that men in couple households with dependent children were more likely than other men to work long hours – more than one-third of these men worked 49 hours a week or more, although after a child's birth, one-quarter of men in work changed their working practices to fit in with this in some way. So on the whole, for those of us in couple relationships with men and children, there is unlikely to be much *practical* support.

Paradoxically, it is often easier to make decisions about the part your children's father can play in their lives when he is not clambering for a high-profile role. If he is away on business for a large part of the time, you know he is a leisure-time father. If you are separated from each other, whoever has custody, and it is usually the mother, then again, the rules and divisions of responsibility are clearly drawn – often formally. The greatest difficulty for Super-woman comes when she shares children with the apparently child-focused man.

When I carried out my study of the transition to motherhood,[13] I asked the women I interviewed about the baby's father and their expectations of the way he

would cope with fatherhood. Nearly all of the women
believed that he would be an equal partner in the infant
care. Nearly all of the first-time mothers, in particular,
were wrong. What I discovered was that:

> *Many men find it difficult to cope. They do not
> expect things to change a great deal for them, and
> it is difficult for many men to explain to friends
> that they can no longer do the social things they
> used to do because they have to take an active
> parenting role.*
>
> *It can be a vicious circle. ... evidence indicates
> that this problem is more widespread than the cov-
> erage by experts has previously indicated.*[14]

Not only do men find the social pressure difficult, because
they have not been brought up to expect what accom-
panies the parenthood role, they also lose intimacy with
their partners in a number of ways that researchers have
found distresses the fathers a great deal. For example,
many women have sexual difficulties in the months after
childbirth, particularly if they have had a vaginal delivery
and had stitches. Women are also very tired and baby-
centred, if they are breastfeeding. In addition, women
frequently find it difficult to feel attractive themselves
(which is an important part of female sexuality), when
they are overweight and sore and feel like a milk-cow –
however much they value their partner and being a
mother. But it's more than sex; women are more likely
to put their energies, time and attention toward the
needs of their child than those of their partner. It makes
perfect sense: the man is an autonomous adult; the baby
cannot survive without a high level of attention. But men
frequently feel misunderstood and neglected when this
happens, and this detracts from their energies and abilities

as fathers. The pressure on new fathers is enormous, and it has increased with the legacy of feminism and the rise of Superwoman. Not only are men not brought up to realise the pressures they are going to face, but often their partners don't recognise them either, because they are so child care focused. I found that women feel very resentful towards the fathers because they feel let down – the men have not met their promises.

*Throughout the discussions with all the women I interviewed, there was an undercurrent of rage. They were angry with the midwives, doctors, hospital policies, way they were treated, their own bodies, their own behaviours, their circumstances, the losses they experienced and their failure to deal with that rage. Far from feeling guilty and a burden to their partners, many of them expressed fury at the man for not being prepared to change while they themselves do the work and make the compromises.*

*Despite the positive view that most of the respondents had had about their partners prior to the birth, there were many ways in which they felt let down by them. Jane's case is typical. She told of a difficult day when she was exhausted because the baby had been particularly tired and irritable. Her fiancé went out for a drink with his friends and did not return till four in the morning. That was the first time. Since then he frequently went out and came home very late, saying that he did not think that the baby should change his life.*

*More subtly, Francis's husband told her she was not a good mother, a role in life she would not have chosen if it had not been for his insistence. He was very good at handling the children and criticised the*

*way she coped with them. This eroded her confi-
dence, which had diminished anyway since the
birth of the second baby.*[15]

Both men and women are under pressure when they
become parents. While women are prepared by health
professionals and by the expectations of motherhood
that they have always had, to anticipate losing sleep and
energy and to put child care first, men are treated differently. The child care experts pay scant attention to the
role of the father. Fathers are expected to provide social
support *for the mother* whereas they themselves have also
undergone a trauma and life change for which they are
probably less well prepared than their partners. This
change in their lives continues for as long as they are responsible for the upbringing and care of their children.
Michael White head of the Policy Studies Institute in the
UK is quoted recently as saying:

*At present we have at best half the ingredients for
women with children to develop a satisfactory
working life. The other half must include shorter
hours for their male partners, so that they can do
more to help at home, and greater equality in pay so
that women do not need to work so long to balance
the household budget.*[16]

The choice to have children with Superwoman, rather
than a woman who is primarily a home-maker, brings
men's lives into the 21st century, and there are few pre-
cedents and role models. Men's learning curve has to be as
steep, if not steeper than their partners'. If men are to
enjoy parenthood, then they need to do more than pay
for the nanny and accept that the mother has primary

child care management responsibility. They need to be more active, to gain a greater balance in *their* lives between work and home.

## Superwoman and the backlash against feminism

It may be ironic, because the majority of Superwomen would probably deny that feminism had anything to do with their lives, but the backlash against feminism has turned against Superwomen too. Superwomen are now increasingly being portrayed as past-tense, '90s' women. Hilary and Rosanna are the image that is being created of the 21st century woman – they recognise what is *really* valuable in life. No more long evenings at the office, no more working at home all through the night. Home, hearth and family come first. But how much of this is choice and responding to what Superwoman needs and wants, and how much is a result of the anti-feminist (and thus anti-woman) backlash.

Susan Faludi identified the emerging backlash 10 years ago:

> *To be a woman at the close of the twentieth century – what good fortune. That's what we keep hearing anyway. The barricades have fallen, politicians assure us. Women have 'made it', the style pages cheer. Women's fight for equality has 'largely been won', Time magazine announces. Enrol at any university, join any law firm, apply for credit at any bank. Women have so many opportunities now, corporate leaders say, that we don't really need equal*

*opportunities policies. Women are so equal now, lawmakers say, that we no longer need equal rights legislation. 'The battle for women's rights has been largely won,' Mrs. Thatcher has proclaimed. The days when they were demanded in strident tones should be gone forever. Even American Express ads have saluted a woman's freedom to charge it. At last women have received their full citizenship papers.*

*And yet ...*

*Behind this celebration of women's victory, behind the news. Cheerfully and endlessly repeated, that the struggle for women's rights is won, another message flashes. You may be free and equal now, it says to women, but you have never been more miserable.*[17]

This is the message for Superwoman – again and again. We are going to sell you a version of yourself that suggests you only have yourself to blame. Women are free and equal so why are you complaining? Why are you not reaching the top and staying there happily? Why are we hearing of women leaving work, demoting themselves or going part-time when they become mothers? If they cannot hack motherhood and the glittering career perhaps there is a biological basis to the glass ceiling? Go back where you belong and leave power, money and influence to men, *because, don't forget, men have managed all this and been fathers for years and years!*

Susan Faludi first identified the backlash message about motherhood versus the glittering career in 1980 when she spotted the following comments on the front page of the *New York Times*.

*MANY YOUNG WOMEN SAY THEY'D
PICK FAMILY OVER CAREER ... . Actually, the 'many' were a few dozen Ivy League
under-graduates who, despite their protestations,
were heading for medical school and fellowships at
Oxford.* The Times *story managed to set off a
brief round of similar back-to-the-home stories in
the press. But with no authority to bless the
trend, returning-to-nesting's future looked
doubtful.*[18]

However, in the 21st century, this backlash promotion has
turned into a well-publicised reality. In April 2002 the
BBC News reported a poll* by *Mother and Baby* magazine
that women are finding it difficult to juggle the demands
of motherhood and a career. The BBC news web site
declared:

*The impact appears to be greatest on women who
leave it until their late 30s to start a family.*

*A poll by* Mother and Baby *magazine has found
that many are struggling to cope on five hours' sleep
a night.*

*The consequent sleep deprivation is playing havoc
with their relationships and working lives.*

*The survey found:*

*56% of working mothers said weariness left them in
a 'state of despair';*

---

* Which was so insignificant in its display that I spent some time
looking at the magazine itself before I could find it.

*82% admitted a lack of sleep affected their perform-
ance at work;*

*88% felt tired and fed up, exhausted and pulled in
too many directions;*

*70% said their tiredness was so debilitating they felt
unable to function properly;*

*61% said their boss was not understanding.*

The piece continued with suggestions that relationships
were breaking down for these women and that exhaustion
made it difficult to be good mothers. After the headlines
though, was the fact that the article was talking about
women who had had their babies very recently and had
returned to high-powered jobs after only a few weeks.
Compare this with someone who had just had a major
operation: they would be advised to take 3 months off
work, and then perhaps return part-time. With a young
baby, the physical effects are often similar, and sometimes
worse. However, instead of recuperative resting, women
are deprived of sleep, learn new skills, and have work and
responsibilities and emotional upheavals that they never
expected.

# Conclusions: You don't need to do it all and you don't need to lose it all!

*Superwoman was a 'construct of guilt and ambiva-
lence, and women were played upon by people not
sympathetic to them,' said Suzanne Braun Levine,
a New York media critic and author of the*

*forthcoming book* The Daddy Track: How Men Are Re-inventing Fatherhood.

   *Many women 'pretended they could do everything, so society wouldn't punish them for having a job'.*[19]

Superwoman needs to make up her own mind regardless of what others are trying to say is good for her. You need to be true to yourself and what you want and need, or else you will be depressed and miserable, and then you will not be good for others, and you certainly won't be good for yourself.

   Balance in your life does not mean having to sacrifice what you want to do – it does not even necessarily mean that you cannot have it all. It probably does mean, though, that you have to see your life in the longer term – that you can have it all, *but not necessarily have it all at once.* You need to consider your health – physical and mental – in a systematic and strategic way. You need to plan your life around the things that you really want and the things that will bring nourishment to the person you are and want to continue to be. You can have children, friends, partner and career – but you want to have them along with your physical health and sanity.

# Coping with stress

*Superwoman says 'No!'*

## Juggle don't struggle!

> *Balancing work with the rest of life is something we*
> *all have to do. And there's no doubt that the way*
> *our working life is organised makes all the differ-*
> *ence to how we manage our lives.*[1]

*Juggle don't struggle* is a new and important message for
Superwoman, proposed recently by the British Government, concerned that we should achieve a good *balance*
between work and the rest of our lives. For this important
message not to be lost it is vital that Superwoman, and
those who live and work with her, understand her psychology. Superwoman is not a *product* of women's
emancipation and increased occupational choices: she is
the *motivator – the driving force. Superwoman is a self-
actualiser* – Superwoman wants to *do* what she can and
*have* what she can. Women all over the world suffer
physically and emotionally if they are constrained in

their human right to live *as they would choose*. Women in some Eastern cultures, such as those living under successive repressive regimes in Afghanistan, are *not* content to be hidden behind the veil. Many are bravely speaking out against their oppressors. Many more are afraid. *All women* want the opportunity to choose where and how they manage their domestic and public lives.

For Superwoman, the dilemmas surround the fact that she is torn between her own expectations and those of the society in which she lives. She suffers the pressures and conflicts related to struggling with the joint demands of work and family life. However, neither work nor home by themselves are easy options for Superwoman. Men have not rolled over and allowed Superwoman into powerful positions without a tussle – sometimes above-board and sometimes underhand! The workplace is hard for Superwoman, even though she enjoys it.

Men have not just given up their *traditional* domestic role as head of the household. Fathers have not taken over equal responsibilities for child care and domestic arrangements. Men have made 'concessions'. Many men have changed their views and behaviours and seen personal and social advantages in those changes. Even more have not – or have made some concessions grudgingly.

Superwoman, therefore, is subject to a great deal of stress at home, at work and in that space between the two where guilt and anxiety creep in. That stress needs to be recognised, understood and managed if she is to exchange the struggling for effective juggling.

## Stress and Superwoman

*in the final analysis, it isn't external events, however hectic or unpleasant, that determine whether we're stressed or not, it's something inside ourselves.*[2]

All of us have stress in our lives. Sometimes it is caused by events such as a death of a close friend, a partner leaving us, ill-health, school-related problems with our children or even something like preparation for a holiday or Christmas. Stressful events such as these (called 'Stressors' by psychologists) happen to us all and there are times when they seem to pile on top of each other through no clear fault of our own or anyone else. The *experience* of stress is within ourselves. You *feel* stress when there are outside pressures – but the feelings may vary in strength, intensity or length of time. The feeling of being stressed comes about in times of crisis, and in times of joy. It is a physical and psychological sense of excitement, challenge and demand. Many of us *enjoy* having stress in our lives – the alternative is grey, dull, boredom. Some people, such as stockmarket traders, and many Superwomen, are likely to be *stress junkies* or, at the very least, to demand that their lives contain some stress-inducing challenges. When your work is so exciting that you want to be working all your waking hours, and want to talk only about work when you are not doing it – and can't wait to get up in the morning (if indeed you have gone to bed) so you can do more of it – that suggests that (for periods of time at least) you *thrive* on stress.

Many of us do thrive on a certain amount of stress – particularly when we are rewarded. When you are making millions of dollars for your company, getting papers published in top academic journals, winning court cases – when you and your skills are in demand and professional rewards and personal plaudits are being showered upon you – why not go on and on? It is exciting, it is a challenge and you are *meeting* the challenges. You feel like Superwoman and want to stay that way forever. However, stress junkies also eventually experience physical and psychological burn-out. Our bodies and minds have not evolved to take long-term excitement and stress. Burn-out results in physical ill-health and depression. Sometimes stress junkies find that once they have been forced into a burn-out related halt in their lives, then eventually they regain their energy and get going again – it becomes a very vicious cycle. But unless we learn to deal more effectively with our stress levels, then we resemble leaking batteries and never recharge properly. The burn-out will arrive more quickly during each cycle, the excitement will only be generated after even greater challenges than previously and long-term satisfaction will gradually be eroded.

Two important factors have to be considered if you are to live your life in a healthy, productive and enjoyable way:

**1** How do you learn to recognise and respond to stress so it doesn't take you by surprise and overwhelm you?

**2** How can you break this stress/burnout cycle?

## Recognising stress in our lives

Stress is about pressure or demands made upon us. Such demands are part of our everyday lives, especially for those of us whose lives are about getting the best out of ourselves – self-actualisers – seeking out such pressures.

Some of us look for athletic or adventurous challenges such as beating sporting records or parachute jumping. Their efforts and the achievements give those who seek them an important *buzz*. That buzz is what makes life worth living. I still recall watching a television documentary, some years ago now, about a rock climber. He never used safety equipment and he would seek more and more difficult rock faces to challenge him, until it looked to me as if he was walking on the ceiling without any physical means of staying up there. He said that he could only be happy if he had these challenges in his life, and he fully expected to die by falling from a rock face. That was OK with him.

As with Superwoman and other self-actualisers, life/work has to be a challenge. You need to test your capacities.

There are two important components of our reactions to stressors – physiological and psychological.

## Physiological response to long-term stress

We have all heard of the fight/flight response in animals and humans: when there is a sign of danger (or stressor), the human body pumps adrenaline triggered by the autonomic nervous system. *It isn't a choice* – the autonomic nervous system goes into this mode automatically. The physiological things that take place all have a purpose in preparation for fight or flight:

- *Adrenaline and noradrenaline are released into the bloodstream* – they stimulate and speed up reflexes and increase metabolic responses, which gives us a short-term burst of energy and heightened awareness.

- If we then go into instant action mode, all returns to normal after the crisis is over; but 21st century work-related stress is frequently not the kind that requires instant action – indeed a fight/flight response is usually counter-productive. Long-term consequences can be cardiovascular disease, strokes, hypertension and other serious medical conditions.

- *Other hormones are then released* from the thyroid gland to enable further energy release from energy stored in the body.

  - If this goes on too long we stand to be exhausted and drained of energy, which may end in physical collapse.

- *Cholesterol is released* from the liver to aid muscle function and then to bring more energy into play.

  - Permanently elevated blood cholesterol is dangerous because it results in hardening of the arteries and heart attacks.

Thus it is possible to see why the stress response in your body might be both addictive and productive – particularly if you are continually under pressure at home and at work. You need to keep going, and you need to draw on energy that you get from your fight/flight responses. However, in the medium to long term you will damage your health. It is also likely that you will damage your emotional health and relationships at home or at work even sooner.

The extreme signs and symptoms of the fight/flight response or 'alarm mode' are:

| Physical reaction | Symptom |
| --- | --- |
| Adrenalin triggered | Headaches, dizziness |
| Pupils dilate | Blurred vision |
| Mouth goes dry | Difficulty swallowing |
| Neck and shoulder muscles tense | Aching neck, backache |
| Breathing becomes faster and shallower so muscles get a greater supply | Chest pains, tingling, asthma |
| Heart pumps faster, blood pressure rises | High blood pressure |
| Liver releases cholesterol | Excess sugar in blood, indigestion |
| Body cools itself and perspires | Excess sweating, blushing |
| Muscles at opening of bladder and anus relaxed | Frequent urination, diarrhoea |

The alarm mode is the way the body seeks out a burst of energy and shuts down unnecessary functions so that a short-term crisis can be faced and overcome.


## Psychological responses to long-term stress

There are three types of psychological responses to too much stress:

- those that affect cognition (or thinking)
- those that affect us emotionally
- those that affect our behaviour

What follows is a list of the symptoms under these three categories and, although we might be able to recognise having experienced some or even many of them, very few of us experience them all, even when we have been extremely stressed. However, all of them have been noted in people under these conditions.

COGNITIVE EFFECTS

- poor concentration and short attention span, diminished powers of observation
- easily distracted – peter out in the middle of a sentence, forget what you went to the cupboard for
- short- and long-term memory deterioration – can't remember names, dates, faces or what you prepared for last night's dinner
- unpredictable response time – less effective on the tasks you otherwise enjoy
- make more mistakes
- don't manage to plan things or organise you daily life – double-book appointments, forget to complete your tax returns, or forget your children's birthdays
- feel a bit out of touch with reality – think people don't like you, misunderstand people, documents and events

EMOTIONAL EFFECTS

- increased physical tension, cannot relax or sleep, anxiety and worries increase
- hypochondria – imagined symptoms occur in addition to the stress responses in the body
- personality changes – for example, you might become aggressive, not interested in work
- interpersonal problems – have arguments which are unnecessary, feel hostile
- depression and despair
- care less about what matters to you
- self-esteem drops – you don't feel like your normal, competent self

BEHAVIOURAL RESPONSES

- problems with speech – less articulate
- less enthusiastic about everything – don't do all the things you would normally do
- absenteeism
- drug abuse
- low energy
- sleep disrupted
- not cooperative or as friendly as usual
- ignore new information, including that which might be helpful
- deal with problems superficially
- shift responsibilities to others
- odd mannerisms may appear – being unpredictable, shouting at people, swearing at them
- suicide threats

This list of psychological symptoms represents those of the severely long-term-stressed person who is facing imminent burn-out. However, even medium-term stress can bring about a large number of these symptoms and, if you are honest with yourself, you might be able to recognise experiencing several of them in the recent past.

# How to cope with stress

Recognising the signs and symptoms of stress at an early stage is a very important means of reducing long-term stress, provided you know what to do once you have recognised it.

Psychological responses to stress are within our own control and we find ways to cope. Some of our *coping mechanisms* are better for us than others. Bad coping mechanisms leave us in a constant state of crisis and effective ones enable us to recognise a potential crisis and deal with it in a way that prevents long-term build-up of stress and its physiological consequences.

To be effective in stress management we have to pay attention to *external* aspects of stress (environmental) and the *internal* (psychological) factors.

## External stress factors

We all have different types of environment to cope with, but for Superwoman the stress is likely to come from pressures at work, worries and pressures at home and the gaps between these two aspects of her life. Liz, the heroine in the novel *Having it All*, provides some good examples of external stress factors to examine.

1 She was a high-powered executive in television and thus also high-profile.

2 She was the only woman in that situation and had other women and some men who were enemies because of that and were looking for ways of under-mining her.

3 She had two young children whom she could only see at weekends as she consistently failed to get home before they were asleep.

4 She had a husband who felt he was being neglected and who she eventually thought was having an affair with one of her closest friends.

**5**  Her nanny was getting stressed because the children wanted their mother and the nanny had no power to get Liz home on time.

**6**  She had a long commute through London from the office to the suburb in which she lived.

**7**  She nearly always had to take work home.

Thus her external stressors were:

- very high workload
- pressure at work to get everything right and maintain an image of competency
- poor communications and hostility from colleagues
- unrealistic demands from her family for her time and energy
- pressure from her nanny to look after her needs as well
- a threat from a close friend in relation to her husband
- unpredictable and stressful journey to and from work
- no separation from office and home because work was done in both; also, phone calls about the children's or her husband's needs intruded into her office time
- *no time to herself to unwind and relax*

But how can Liz cope with all these stresses? There doesn't seem to be any answer. Remembering that here we are only thinking about the external or environmental stressors, there are a number of strategies that she can employ.

**1** *She can start to identify them* – this may sound a bit over-simplified, but just recognising that *certain things are stressful* and that they are *external* is helpful.

**2** Once she has identified them, *she can place them in categories* of stressfulness. Thus she might say that commuting is stressful and happens regularly, but her fears about her relationship with her husband are more important, and potentially more significant.

**3** She can develop a strategy for reducing and managing the stressors. For example, for some she might be able to *ignore or adapt*, for others she can *act on immediately* and yet others she can *begin to think about*.

  – *Ignore or adapt to*: envious colleagues, maintaining the image of competency. Adapt to being the object of envy and be wary of other colleagues because of that. Remember that being perfect is impossible, so don't try.
  – *Immediate action*: commuting – she can either have a company car to collect her and take her home or she can arrange to do some of her work at home during the day via the plethora of IT that is now available – e-mail, telephone and visual telephone conferencing, for instance.
  – *Begin to think about* – relationships at home. She needs to talk to her husband and nanny. Solutions here are longer-term. The children are not hers alone. If the weekend is the time she is best able to spend with the children, then her husband and the nanny (who is after all paid to do the job that Liz wants her to do) have to

enable her to be physically and mentally able to see them at weekends.

## Internal stress factors

Certain events and environmental factors produce a stress reaction in most people (e.g. unreliable commuting, bereavement). However, in other cases some people get stressed and others not (or at least not so much). These include facing exams or interviews, chairing meetings, appearing on the television, giving a public talk, being criticised, having a difficult boss or colleague or meeting new people. The impact that each potential stressor has upon each of us varies according to:

- the degree to which particular circumstances make us anxious
- how we manage that anxiety and 'where it comes from'
- the type of person we are
- the way we see the world around us and our own place in the world
- how we perceive our rights and roles in dealing with stressors

There are numerous psychological explanations and approaches to dealing with stress, and the way that they are described depends upon the theoretical preferences of the psychologist advancing the approach.

In the case of helping Superwoman maintain her health under stress, I am going to focus on three main psychological characteristics that need to be understood in order to manage the way stress impacts upon you:

*personality type, the role of anxiety in your life* and *self-esteem.*

PERSONALITY

It is difficult to define personality because psychologists often take different approaches to whether personality is 'stable' and enduring or whether it is genetic or environmental. These major issues have not been fully resolved as yet. Earlier in the book I discussed preferences and types that distinguish between individuals and enable us to predict which kinds of people are better at doing different things with a view to helping people make choices that suit their own preference and personality type. There is a well-defined set of behavioural characteristics that some psychologists have identified to predict who might become ill under external pressures. It is known as the Type A personality.

Type A individuals are competitive, driven, impatient and inflexible. They are very invested and involved in their work, they like deadlines and other pressures, they prefer to lead rather than be led, they are more anxious for approval by seniors than by peers or junior colleagues and they are intolerant of weakness in themselves or others. They can be described therefore as:

> *Easily bored, guilty when relaxing, characteristically doing several things at once, focused on their own interests, doing most things at top speed, tense, enjoying winning, and pushing their children, partners and colleagues towards achievement.*

Like all psychological assessments of this kind, few of us will say this describes us absolutely, but many will admit to having some of these tendencies. You wouldn't be Superwoman if you did not share some of these traits!

As Type A personalities are most at risk of high blood pressure, heart attacks and reduced immunities, it is worthwhile trying to change some of those characteristics where possible. It is important for Type A individuals to recognise that they are causing themselves harm and then to consider what can be changed at relatively little personal cost.

Greater awareness of others' needs and your own need for rest and relaxation are important, along with developing more patience and trust towards and in yourself and others.

It is not an easy undertaking to change habits such as these that are so ingrained in our vision of who we think we are; but it is important, if you are to survive and continue to be effective.

ANXIETY

We all understand the feelings which are called anxiety – they are physiologically similar to the fight/flight or alarm reactions – but anxiety itself is more complicated. Anxiety exists in our unconscious memory as well as being part of our reaction to outside stress. It is normal to be anxious about a job interview, or about giving birth, but some people get so anxious that they set themselves up to fail the interview or not cope with the birth without a great deal of distress. The reason for this is that there are at least two aspects of anxiety that we experience every time we are stressed:

**1**  *real or responsive anxiety*, for example that we won't win that contract, or we won't meet a deadline;

**2** an *irrational anxiety* that cannot be explained by the facts of what are happening and what you know about your own skills. This is often called 'free-floating anxiety' and is just that. A person who is characteristically anxious becomes anxious for no reason *on top of or in addition to the real anxiety* produced by what is happening at the time. This anxiety is unpredictable and out of control, and for those who experience it, it is totally overwhelming.

The causes of irrational and free-floating anxiety are described by the psychoanalytic theorists Freud and Melanie Klein.[3] Free-floating anxiety, very simply, comes about because insecurities in infancy were not resolved. This may be because parents did not *contain* the anxieties for the infant/child by soothing and reassuring them. But also because they might have been the cause of them. Thus a child whose parents were insecure themselves about infant and child care would pass on a sense of anxiety to the child, as well as stimulate the infant/child's natural anxiety about ensuring they obtained what they needed for life – such as nourishment.

This type of anxiety can be resolved: either by a good experience of healing, love and affection in which the individual experiences that free-floating anxiety as containable, and thus not overwhelming and out of their control, or by a psychotherapeutic experience with a similar outcome. If, however, the free-floating anxiety is not understood and resolved, it can be a major source of distress and disempowerment particularly when accompanied by the Superwoman lifestyle.

SELF-ESTEEM

High self-esteem is important for Superwoman – if we

don't think well of ourselves then it is difficult to think well of others and easy to feel anxious and bad about how they see us. It has been suggested by several writers that 'wanting to have it all' is caused by low self-esteem and that 'being seen to achieve' is compensation. Of course, other writers like Abraham Maslow recognise that some people with a good sense of self-esteem behave in a similar way. The jury is out. But, like many other things, our psychological responses often provide us with conflicts and mixtures of emotions and thoughts. One thing is for sure: that prolonged and damaging amounts of stress ultimately reduce self-esteem because our bodies and minds suffer.

## Breaking the stress/burn-out cycle?

It is not easy to break the cycle, although one of the most important predictors is whether or not you recognise and admit to suffering negatively from stress. Once you have recognised the impact of stress on your mind and body, then the next stage is to resolve to change things. This may sound trite, but we don't always resolve to diet even when we are aware of and upset about putting on weight. We need to shift ourselves into the frame of mind that enables us to change. Once that has happened there are five ways in which you can help yourself.

**1** *Rethinking your thinking* – or cognitive change techniques. Remembering that stressful events in themselves don't pile on the negative stress without our help – then it makes sense that, if you change the way you think about what happens to you, even if it

is only a little, then the level of stress you experience
will reduce. Thus:

- Focus on positive rather than negative events in
  your day, the week, your life. *Remember that even
  though you were chasing deadlines all day, that
  even though your colleagues did not seem to be
  pulling their weight, and that even though your
  youngest child was sent home from nursery with a
  temperature and the nanny was phoning you in a
  panic ... you also read a brilliant review of your
  latest book!* For those of us who succumb to
  negative stressors, we often don't have time to
  think about the good things that are happening
  to us because it seems that it is negative ones that
  need attention.
- Don't dwell on things. *What do you do if you find
  a colleague has been 'bad mouthing' you and you
  had trusted them? Deal with it and move on – you
  can't change what they have done and said by
  dwelling on their treachery!* Some people experience upsets, antagonism, humiliation, resent-
  ments and then move on immediately – others
  carry them around with them for ages, and
  they eat away at your body and soul. Don't
  cling on.
- Don't regret how you might have handled things
  differently once the time for action has passed. It
  will do you no good – if it is appropriate learn
  from your mistakes, but don't continue to rebuke
  yourself. You will simply pile on the stress to no
  avail.

**2** *Make sure you have time to yourself* each day for
relaxation and reflection – even if it is the time it
takes you to have a relaxing bath. Don't let anyone

interrupt you. You need and deserve to have your own time, however short.

**3** *Do things to heal your body* – meditation, yoga, swimming, running or going to the gym. And teach yourself to enjoy whatever you choose to do.

**4** *Improve your diet* – cut out or cut down on alcohol, cigarettes, coffee, tea, fatty foods, sugar, salt, meat. Have lots of water, fruit and vegetables. However, if you enjoy chocolate or coffee, for example, stop and savour what you eat or drink. Enjoy them.

**5** *Listen to your self.* Practice thinking about what *you* need and want from each situation – at home and at work. Don't be so busy that you are pushed from pillar to post meeting everyone else's needs – even though you are so good at it. You may be out of training in thinking of what you want. Try harder! If you feel angry or sad, admit it and express it in some way. Find someone else to talk to – a friend or even a therapist. In between times, keep a diary of your feelings about various events and experiences and try to learn lessons for the future from your reactions in the past. *All these things take practice, time and motivation – but they could be life-saving.*

## Assertiveness – saying 'no'

*Assertive behaviour means standing up for your personal rights, and expressing your thoughts, feelings and beliefs in direct, honest and helpful ways, which do not violate the rights of others.*

*Assertiveness means respecting yourself, expressing your needs, and defending your rights. It also means respecting the needs, feelings and rights of other people.*[4]

There are three types of behaviour that people adopt when under pressure. These are passive, aggressive or assertive, and it is only with the last that long-term stress in relationships might be avoided. The other two lead to poor relationships and the build-up of bad feelings, lack of trust in yourself and others and thus negative stress in time.

- *Passive behaviour* occurs when you avoid saying what you want to say and fail to express how you feel. It can lead to feeling anxious, ignored, hurt and later resentful.
- *Aggressive behaviour* occurs when you act at the expense of others in some way.
- *Assertive behaviour* occurs when you can honestly say what you want and need but respect others' needs as well.

Becoming assertive is another recognised technique of stress management – although it may seem a bit of a tautology to suggest that Superwoman needs to be assertive. However, in learning to juggle not struggle, you need to recognise how you might have been agreeing to the demands of others without thinking about it. And because you have always said 'yes' in the past, then they have always expected you to carry on responding to them in that way, even though your burdens have increased and theirs have not.

Rhoda, always did her mother-in-law, May's, shopping when she did her own. That involved not only the trip to the supermarket, but also dropping it off at May's house, helping her put the things away, staying for a cup of tea and doing any odds and ends that she was asked to do. She liked May, but the routine of this was beginning to interfere with her own working and domestic schedules as, over the years, Rhoda had become a partner in her law firm and also a mother. The reason for this habit in the first place was that May didn't drive. While she wanted to continue a close relationship with May she had to find a way of telling her to do her own shopping, even offering to pay the taxi fare, without appearing to be hostile and rejecting. She managed to do this in the end after much agonising, very simply by telling May the truth, making sure that she came to the family home for dinner at least once a week and finding that May and she enjoyed each other's company even more when Rhoda was not experiencing May as a burden. That sounds so simple – and yet we build up a whole host of reasons why we should not 'let others down' or hurt them, when in fact the person we are hurting the most is often ourself.

Debbie was furious when she learned that a junior colleague had complained to her boss that she was exploiting her assistants. The colleague had not handled the situation at all well, and had written a poorly constructed letter of complaint about Debbie rather than attempting to express her discontent to Debbie herself in the first place. However, having had some training in assertiveness, instead of venting her rage on the colleague and to her boss, she called them both to a meeting telling them how she respected the problems they might face in the company from carrying out their respective roles, and that she herself was under pressure. She suggested that they consider some of the junior colleagues' anxieties and then find a way to move forward. From that point on the junior colleague felt able to bring her problems to Debbie, rather than going above her, and a mutual respect developed. Debbie was also able to learn about how some aspects of her behaviour were seen by her staff – things that she hadn't realised appeared to be dismissive or aggressive.

You need to develop your assertiveness if the following things describe some of your behaviours:

- You sometimes fail to draw lines, set limits, speak up or say 'no' to people who make demands on you.
- You sometimes think you are responding to other people's priorities above your own.
- You sometimes feel that the only way to get your own needs met and to avoid being at the beck and call of those around you is to fight back.
- You sometimes feel that if you didn't look after everyone else's needs you would be a failure as a lover, friend, mother or colleague and that they would leave, ignore or overlook you.

Being assertive is a useful way of dealing with external pressures that add negative stress to your life because it enables you to set limits on how much and how often other people can make demands on you without making you feel guilty. It helps to boost self-esteem in the long run because it enables your relationships to become more equal (i.e. give and take rather than you giving and others taking) and for you to feel that others seek your skills and company because of their value rather than because you are a soft touch.

## Conclusions

Will it ever be possible to achieve balance in our lives? How can you juggle home and work so that no-one

| People / Situation | Relatives | Friends | Strangers, tradesmen, shop assistants | Authority figures | Subordinates | Nannies and cleaners | Meetings at work |
|---|---|---|---|---|---|---|---|
| Refusing requests | | | | | | | |
| Handling criticism | | | | | | | |
| Receiving from others | | | | | | | |
| Stating your rights and needs | | | | | | | |
| Giving negative feedback | | | | | | | |
| Expressing negative feelings | | | | | | | |
| Differing with others | | | | | | | |
| Making requests | | | | | | | |
| Expressing positive feelings | | | | | | | |
| Making social contacts | | | | | | | |

**Figure 9** How often are you assertive? (Adapted from Charlesworth and Nathan (1993, p. 210).[4])

suffers – even and especially you? *It is clear that you cannot have it all, all of the time.* Balance is about not having it all at once. Balance is about being yourself – and the *development* of your self is an ongoing *process* in your life. How do we achieve self-development that leads to health and balance?

The first lesson, *understanding and caring for yourself,* may be the most important, and the most difficult for Superwoman. Some people think that being Superwoman is all about self – you know it is not. It is about *doing your best* and ensuring that *you look after the people you love the most.* Being Superwoman and having it all is almost self-less – it is disregarding your self, in order to do what you feel you need to do to achieve. It may sound like a riddle – but it is indeed the case that the glittering career and the family life all demand the *sacrifice of your self* in order to be Superwoman. For many Superwomen, day-to-day living consists of *crisis management.* Getting through yet another day without a major disaster at the office and with your children and partner safely in bed represents another success. That sounds bleak – and it isn't the whole story, or you would probably be joining the ranks of those retreating back into the home.

# Challenging choices

*Working with what you've got*

Throughout the 20th century women have been told that
*they have a problem*. This assertion has come from
'experts' such as Freud who said that women presented
him with a 'puzzle'; it has come from the popular media
who discuss and refuel the 'battle between the sexes'; from
writers such as Betty Friedan and Marilyn French who
identified the problem with no name – depression and
loneliness of the affluent housewife/mother; from feminists who challenge society to ensure women's equality at
work; from those who have identified a backlash against
women's equality; from those who are confused about
how men and women should handle their relationships;
and from researchers and politicians concerned to ensure
that families can cope with contemporary life in a stress-
free and health-enhancing way.

As the second half of the 20th century wore on, women
were increasingly motivated towards having it all because
they saw the opportunities. They could enter professions
and the commercial world *and succeed*. They were also
able to marry and have children. Men no longer avoided

relationships with successful women – in fact intelligent and powerful women replaced passive subservient women as symbols of sexual and emotional attractiveness. Women's increased success meant affluence, autonomy, self-confidence and an enhanced self-image. The taste of success increased their motivation to have it all.

## So who has problems now?

In the 21st century, however, women's success was accompanied by the appeal to *put an end to having it all*. This call apparently came from women, but was backed very strongly by the men who control the print, broadcast and cinematic media. The message to women challenged the *femininity* of Superwoman – as a mother, lover and career success. The challenge goes as follows:

- Can Superwoman have a career if it means she is *neglecting* her children? Studies about poor school achievement or stress among young children and adolescents pointed the finger of blame at *mothers*. Mothers would naturally be good at their mothering tasks if only they stuck to them and didn't try to have careers as well. Forget the numerous women of two generations ago who populated the psychiatric hospitals, popped Librium and took their own lives. Forget the evidence that depressed, housebound, un-fulfilled mothers have little left for their children. Forget all the research that shows that children benefit from having relationships with their fathers as well as their mothers – if the father is only seen after bath-time, so be it, he has more important things to do, it is natural. Absent fathers don't cause damage.

- Can Superwoman succeed in the world of men without 'becoming' a man? Kingsley Browne[1] argues that there is no glass ceiling – inequalities in the workplace and the lack of women at the top reflect the fact that men are hard-wired to be more competitive than women – a characteristic passed down from our ancient predecessors. Risk-taking unites the successful hunter and the chief executive. Women are not born to take risks, are thus not born to lead, and if they do so they are going against nature. If they succeed in their careers against the odds, then we *know* they develop higher levels of testosterone, become more aggressive and more like a man. Go against nature at your peril.

- Can Superwoman get and keep a man? Not if you take the media fantasies of Ally McBeal or Bridget Jones seriously. Successful career women have friends and even lovers – but they don't get what they want. They want babies, husbands, houses, white weddings, dishwashers and to live happily ever after. Women are constantly worried about their biological clocks – not only because of the reduction in their fertility as time passes. They are also worried about their looks – and we have the dramatic increase in the take-up of cosmetic surgery to prove this. If we don't care for our appearance we are on the 'scrap heap' and that heap is defined by whether or not we can attract *and keep* a man. We used to think that Sophia Loren, Lauren Bacall, Barbara Castle* and Jane Fonda were great role models – they aged with beauty and grace. Now,

---

* The British politician who died in 2002 while in her nineties.

we need to hide every wrinkle and strand of grey hair. We know that Cher has rejuvenated her appearance so frequently that it is difficult to recognise the woman of today from her 10-year-old movies. Although Elizabeth Taylor has allowed the appearance of grey hair, there is little other evidence of her ageing, even though she is almost the same age as the Queen of England. You can't care about your looks and your career. To succeed in a career you need to look as if you are serious. If you look too serious you won't get your man – and that is what you really wanted all along, isn't it?

- Is Superwoman the product of a screwed-up, politically correct society? If all else fails and women look as if they are having it all, then resort to science. A recent BBC radio discussion stimulated by the thoughts of a male educationalist, Professor Tooley, suggested that the politically correct educational systems that have developed in North America and in north-west Europe have failed girls by denying them the chance to learn domestic skills. He harks back to the time when boys did metalwork and girls did cookery and sewing (called domestic science!). Then we knew where we were and knew our places. He *knows* that the emphasis on academic subjects in schools has not been good for girls because just look at all those unhappy women around trying to have it all. Get back to cleaning the toilet! Tooley's thesis of course is far more to do with worries about boys and men and *their* failures than it is about concern for women's mental health.

The back cover of a popular book about men (*Why Men Don't Iron*)[2] states:

*Why are men at the moment in trouble? Boys are failing at school, men are unable to get jobs, males feel redundant among women.*

The answer provided in that book is that it is *women who are to blame* for men's distress. Women no longer have to depend on men for economic support. Women achieve in their own right. Women can multitask. Emotional intelligence in management is increasingly valued over risk-taking and aggression. Women are the ones who manage the home and thus are most often the ones to whom the children turn in times of distress. Women are more likely to get custody of their children, following divorce, than are men. Men need to be looked after and, if they are widowed or divorced, are more likely to remarry. Women, after a life of marriage, are more likely to enjoy living on their own. Women like sex – they are not just male conquests. Women care for their health while men's health is a major public health concern. Women find it easy to make friends while men are increasingly emotionally isolated.

## Women joining in

But there is little joy in *having it all* at the expense of other human beings. There is no great pleasure in winning the 'battle' of the sexes and destroying the 'opposition'. That does not make the world a better place for women or for men. Health and happiness are a product of negotiated mutual support and harmony. It is increasingly men who have problems – and in their panic they try to make women, and the opportunities that have been opened up to us, responsible for what they themselves are losing.

But some women are eager to join in others' attempts to demolish what we have achieved. While it is clearly time to rethink how we organise our lives – it should not be the time to throw away what feminism has accomplished. *Having* it all, for many, *has* meant *doing* it all. This has perhaps hindered the achievement of happiness and fulfilment; but were we happy and fulfilled when we were chained to the kitchen sink? Not according to Betty Friedan and the other commentators from pre-liberation days.

The problems for today's Superwoman, as summarised by Danielle Crittenden, seem to be as follows:

*In a way, the situation women wake up in today is more dire than the one of thirty years ago when Friedan first sat down to write about the gnawing 'problem with no name'. For unlike the problem about which Friedan spoke – which afflicted educated suburban wives trapped and unfulfilled in their well-upholstered ranch homes – this new problem with no name affects the female executive high atop the city in her glass office as much as the single mother struggling to lift a stroller onto a bus thirty stories below. Despite sweeping government programmes, tens of billions of dollars in social spending, and massive social upheaval in the name of sexual equality, you only have to glance through a newspaper or switch on the news to be subject to a litany of gloomy statistics about today's women: We are more likely to be divorced or never married at all than women of previous generations. We are more likely to bear children out of wedlock. We are more likely to be junkies or die in poverty.*

*We are more likely to have an abortion or catch a sexually transmitted disease. If we are mothers, even of infants and very small children, we are more likely to work at full-time jobs and still shoulder the bulk of housework as well.*[3]

This clearly has some truth for some women. These statistics need qualification, though. Perhaps more women are getting divorced today because they are more able to do so – the legal and economic opportunities for leaving a bad marriage have improved women's lives. The increase in poverty, abortion, disease and illegal, addictive and dangerous drugs are features of society. Western industrial societies are less regulated than they were 20 years ago. Thatcher and Reagan drove us further towards the 'me' societies. We no longer care about those less able or fortunate than ourselves. We don't care to educate the lower social classes – we don't teach them history. Many of today's Superwomen have never heard of Betty Friedan anyway – so how do we know that women in earlier generations were depressed, hospitalised, brutalised and pathologised? Today many men and women know that if they don't succeed quickly, make money, get ahead, have a family – it could be taken away. Most high-flyers are burnt out in their thirties. There is little compassion and little knowledge of what the recent past held and what we as women and men have escaped to get where we are today.

*The Times* newspaper (of London) recently ran a series of articles suggesting that women should plan their babies as carefully as their careers.[4] This also means that:

*. . . if you're to beat the biological clock, you must find a partner before you turn 30.*

Hewlett here makes the important point that most high-achieving women are childless and frequently single, because having it all is very difficult. Often in order to achieve serious success, you need to reach a relatively high career stage before you are 35. This has typically disadvantaged women currently in their fifties and sixties because they did not have the opportunities when they were young – the world has opened up for women relatively recently. Hewlett[4] points out:

> *Established professionals are quite clear in their advice to this generation: postpone childbearing as long as you can and there will be a huge payoff in the workplace. Distressingly, this expert advice is extremely sound: motherhood does derail and destroy careers and needs to be avoided if a young woman wants to get a career off the ground in optimal fashion.*

She argues that you need to plan the way to finding your man and having children in the way that you would also plan your career. It is also important to choose a profession that is forgiving of age without rigid career/age trajectories. 'Choose a company that will help you to achieve work/life balance.' In the end, her message is: *if your timing and strategy are right, grab what you can and have it all.*

## Choices for today's Superwoman

If we want it all, the decision of how to manage our lives comes back to us. We may find a way of navigating through a minefield and finding the right men, the right careers and the right companies to work for – life will still be hard though. There may be little time and energy left over for the extra burdens that hit you in the face when you need them the least. How do you cope when the nanny gets ill or, worse, leaves? How do you manage your work if you have additional stress at home? How do you cope with the pressure at home if you are being harassed or pressurised at work? What happens if you get ill?

We desperately need to be asking different questions from those asked by Crittenden and Tooley and the others who want women to return to the never-existent domestic bliss. We don't need to focus on happiness – that is more elusive than the popular imagination and media would have us believe. We need to make choices at every stage. We need to be in touch with our histories – as women and individuals. Listen to your body and your emotions. Be self-confident and self-aware. Think about what you want to do for yourself and what you need to do it. Remember at every stage you have a choice. Women's lives provide far more freedom and opportunities than ever before – use them wisely and kindly. Beware and take care of your self and those you care about, and spend time reflecting on what that means and how you can achieve that day by day.

Susie Orbach[5] reminds us that we now live in the age of emotional literacy. That has to advantage us as women for, whatever the rationale, we handle emotions better than men do. Emotional literacy means *recognising and responding* to our emotions. It also means taking *responsibility* for what we want, how we feel and what we do. We can make up our minds about the extent to which we have it all. We need to practise what Orbach calls the three Rs: *registering* our emotions, *recognising* them and querying our initial emotional *responses*:

- we register that something has touched us in a particular way
- then we name the emotional response
- finally we work out whether what we feel is the whole story, or whether more complex emotions are embedded within our response

We have to make choices related to our characteristic temperaments, our preferences and our real rather than our false selves. We need to be true to ourselves and find our own ways of survival. We need to re-evaluate the meaning of having it all, and we can achieve this if we listen carefully to who we really are.

# Further information

- **The Work/Life Balance** web site has ideas about how to achieve a greater balance. It has examples of company schemes for job-sharing and tele-working, and companies who enable employees to set out their own work regimes. It also has case studies of different individuals who have found a way to achieve a better balance.

  The address is:
  http://www.dti.gov.uk/work-lifebalance

- **The Parent Company** in the UK runs seminars on parenting-related topics. In August 2000 there was a seminar on 'Parenting Matters at Work – Finding the Home Work Balance', reported on the web site:

  http://www.ukparents.co.uk/archives/parenting_
    work.shtml

  The telephone number is: +207-935-9635.

- **The Lifewise: Sanity Saver** web-page has a number of simple suggestions to sustain your sanity when you feel you are struggling rather than juggling:

http://www.canoe.ca/LifewiseSanitySaver/
   home.html

- The MBTI is not available to the public but details of how and where you might get assessed can be obtained from: Oxford Psychologists Press, Lambourne House, 311–321, Banbury Road, Oxford, OX2 7JH, UK (telephone: +1865-510203); and CAPT (Centre for Applications of Psychological Type), 2720, NW 6th Street, Gainesville, Florida, USA (telephone: +800-777-2248).

# Notes and references

## Introduction

1  A quotation from Betty Ford taken from *Women's Thoughts*, collected by Helen Exley, New York: Exley Giftbooks, 1996.
2  Germaine Greer, *The Whole Woman*, London: Anchor, 2000, p. 152.
3  http://news.bbc.co.uk/hi/english/uk/newsid_616000/616129.stm
4  http://news.bbc.co.uk/hi/english/business/newsid_1530000/1530355.stm
5  Shirley Conran is currently Chair of the Work–Life Balance Trust and a UK Government ministerial adviser.
6  Article by Elizabeth Gleik in the *New York Times*, January 31st 1999, critically reviewing Crittenden's book published in 1999 by Simon & Schuster in New York.

## Chapter 1

1  Kelly Legge, 'I am Superwoman, hear me roar!' html.www.familysauraus/articles/

2 Diana Mather, *ImageWorks for Women: Make Your Image Work for You*, London: HarperCollins, 1996, p. xi.
3 Sarah Kilby, *Juggling it all: The SHE Guide to Your Work, Your Children, Your Life*, London: Vermillion, 1992, p. vii.
4 G. Brown and C. Brady, *Getting to the Top*, London: Kogan Page, 1991, p. 11.
5 Shirley Conran, *Down with Superwoman: For Everyone Who Hates Housework*, London: Sidgwick & Jackson, 1990, p. 4.
6 The 'Marie Claire interview' with Nicole Kidman, UK edition, September 2001, p. 66.

# Chapter 2

1 Robert Uhlig, 'Superwoman's weakness exposed', http://www.dadi.org/superwoman.htm (2001).
2 Quote from the author Erica Jong in *Women's Thoughts*, collected by Helen Exley, New York: Exley Giftbooks, 1996.
3 Elizabeth Perle McKenna, *When Work Doesn't Work Anymore: Women Work and Identity*, London: Pocket Books, 1997, p. 13.
4 Anne Campbell, *A Mind of Her Own: The Evolutionary Psychology of Women*, Oxford: Oxford University Press, 2002.
5 R. Rapoport and R. Rapoport, *Dual Career Families Re-examined*, London: Martin Robertson, 1976.
6 Alice Lagnado, *The Times Magazine*, 6th April 2002, p. 12.
7 This is the preamble to an article called 'Super Shar' in the UK edition of *Marie Claire*, December 2001, p. 76.
8 This precedes a piece in the same issue (December 2001) of *Marie Claire*; this one is entitled 'I'm not Superwoman', p. 157.
9 These women are the wives of John F. Kennedy, President of the USA, John Major and Harold Wilson, British Prime Ministers during the 1990s and 1970s respectively.
10 Germaine Greer, *The Whole Woman*, London: Anchor, 2000, p. 1.
11 This is from a 'backlash' web site comprising an advert for a tote bag with the logo 'Superwoman Quits to become OWEG' which stands for 'ordinary woman with an extraordinary God'.
12 Germaine Greer in *The Change*, Harmondsworth: Penguin, 1992.

13  Adam Jukes, *Why Men Hate Women*, London: Free Association Books, 1994.
14  Jane Ussher, *Women's Madness: Misogyny or Mental Illness?*, Hemel Hempstead: Harvester Wheatsheaf, 1991, p. 3.
15  Elaine Showalter, *The Female Malady*, London: Virago, 1996, p. 250.
16  Sandra Bem, 'The measurement of clinical androgyny', *Journal of Consulting and Clinical Psychology*, **42**, 155–162 (1974).
17  Denise Riley, *The War in the Nursery*, London: Virago, 1983, p. 189.

# Chapter 3

1  Dorothy Rowe, *The Successful Self: Freeing our Hidden Inner Strengths*, London: HarperCollins, 1993, p. 21.
2  Richard Kwiatowski and Dave Hogan, 'Group membership', in R. Bayne, P. Nicolson and I. Horton (Eds), *Counselling and Communication Skills for Medical and Health Practitioners*, Leicester: BPS Books, 1998.
3  Abraham Maslow, *The Farther Reaches of Human Nature*, Harmondsworth: Penguin, 1977.
4  Carol R. Rogers, *Becoming a Person: A Therapist's View of Psychotherapy*, London: Constable, 1967/2002.
5  Abraham Maslow, *The Farther Reaches of Human Nature*, Harmondsworth: Penguin, 1977, p. 365.
6  Ibid., p. 42.
7  Rowan Bayne, *The Myers–Briggs Type Indicator: A Critical Review and Practical Guide*, London: Chapman & Hall, 1995.
8  Ibid., p. 4.
9  Dorothy Rowe, *The Successful Self: Freeing our Hidden Inner Strengths*, London: HarperCollins, 1993, p. 38.

# Chapter 4

1  http://www.arlenetaylor.org/seminars/superwoman_syndrome. htm

2  http://dadi.org/superwoman.htm
3  Wysiwyg://43/http://ordinarywoman.com/superwoman.html
4  For a comprehensive and clear guide to the MBTI and the theory
   of psychological type, see Rowan Bayne, *The Myers–Briggs Type
   Indicator: A Critical Review and Practical Guide*, London:
   Chapman & Hall, 1995.

# Chapter 5

1  Jean Baker-Miller, *Towards a New Psychology of Women*,
   Harmondsworth: Penguin, 1978, p. 103.
2  Jane Ussher, *Fantasies of Femininity: Reframing the Boundaries of
   Sex*, Harmondsworth: Penguin, 1997, p. 21.
3  M. Maguire, *Men, Women, Passion and Power: Gender Issues in
   Psychotherapy*, London: Routledge, 1995, p. 1.
4  S. Freud, 'Femininity', Lecture 33 in *New Introductory Lectures
   in Psychoanalysis*, Vol. 2, Harmondsworth: Penguin, 1973,
   p. 167.
5  Matina Horner, 'Follow-up studies on the motive to avoid success
   in women', Symposium presentation to the American
   Psychological Association, Miami, Florida, 1970, p. 1.
6  http://www.nih.gov/news/NIH-Record/01_23_2001/
   story04.htm
7  http://womanthink.com/superwoman.htm
8  Wysiwyg://43/http://ordinarywoman.com/superwoman.html
9  S. Freud, 'Femininity', Lecture 33 in *New Introductory Lectures
   in Psychoanalysis*, Vol. 2, Harmondsworth: Penguin, 1973,
   pp. 147–148.
10 Ibid., p. 146.
11 Ibid.
12 Anne Campbell, *A Mind of Her Own: The Evolutionary
   Psychology of Women*, Oxford: Oxford University Press, 2002,
   p. 34.
13 Deborah Tannen, *Talking from Nine to Five*, London: Virago,
   1996, pp. 21–22.
14 Daniel Goleman, *Working with Emotional Intelligence*, London:
   Bloomsbury, 1999, p. 3.

15  Ibid.


# Chapter 6


1  J. Prather, 'Why can't women be more like men?', in L. S. Fidell
   and J. Delameter (Eds), *Women in the Professions: What's All the
   Fuss About?*, London: Sage, 1971, p. 20.
2  Pru  Goward,  Federal  Sex  Discrimination  Commissioner,
   Sydney, Australia, in a speech to the Australian Human Rights
   and Equal Opportunities Commission, November, 2001. http://
   hreoc.gov.au/speeches/sex_discrim/motherlinc_lunch.html
3  *Women  at  the  Top*,  London:  The  Hansard  Society  for
   Parliamentary Government, 1990, p. 15.
4  Karen Ross, *Women at the Top 2000: Cracking the Public Sector
   Glass Ceiling*, London: Hansard Society, 2000, p. 1, quoting from
   *Women  at  the  Top*,  London:  The  Hansard  Society  for
   Parliamentary Government, 1990.
5  *Times Higher Education Supplement*, January 11, 2002, p. 22.
6  H. Marshall and P. Nicolson, 'Why choose psychology? Mature
   and other students accounts at graduation', in J. Radford (Ed.),
   *The Choice of Psychology*, Vol. 12, Occasional Paper, Leicester:
   British Psychological Society, 1991, p. 27.
7  http://www.dti.gov.uk/work-lifebalance/kf.hjt
8  H. Gavron, *The Captive Wife*, Harmondsworth: Penguin, 1966/
   1977; A. Oakley, *Housewife: High Value, Low Cost*, Harmondsworth: Penguin, 1976.
9  C. Kagan and S. Lewis, 'Transforming psychological practice',
   *Australian Psychologist*, **25**, 270–281.
10 http://healthjournal.ucdavis.edu/nov_dec_00_hj/articles/super-
   woman.html A feature appeared on this site by Sue Barton, a
   psychologist with the Department of Family and Community
   Medicine at UC Davis Medical Centre, entitled 'Beware the
   perils of Superwoman syndrome'.
11 B. White, C. Cox and C. Cooper, *Women's Career Development: A
   Study of High-Flyers*, Oxford: Blackwell Business, 1992.
12 Ibid., p. 228.
13 http://womanthink.com/superwoman.htm

14  Cary Cooper and Marilyn Davidson, *High Pressure: Working Lives of Women Managers*, Glasgow: Fontana, 1982.
15  N. V. Benokraitis and J. R. Feagin, *Modern Sexism: Blatant, Subtle and Covert Discrimination*, 2nd edn, New York: Prentice Hall, 1995, p. 59.
16  C. A. MacKinnon, *Sexual Harassment of Working Women*, London: Yale University Press, 1979, p. 18.
17  N. Wolf, *The Beauty Myth*, London: Vintage, 1991, p. 27.
18  C. A. MacKinnon, *Sexual Harassment of Working Women*, London: Yale University Press, 1979.
19  C. Kagan and S. Lewis, 'Transforming psychological practice', *Australian Psychologist*, **25**, 270–281, 1990.
20  P. Carter and T. Jeffs, 'The Don Juans', *Times Higher Educational Supplement*, 10th March, 1995, p. 17.
21  M. Carroll, in C. Morris, *Bearing Witness: Sexual Harassment and Beyond. Everywoman's Story*, New York: Little Brown, 1994, p. 65.
22  D. E. Smith, 'A peculiar eclipsing: Women from men's culture', *Women's Studies International Quarterly*, **1**, 281–295 (1978).

# Chapter 7

1  H. Beckett, 'Cognitive developmental theory in the study of adolescent development', in S. Wilkinson (Ed.), *Feminist Social Psychology: Developing Theory and Practice*, Milton Keynes: Open University Press, 1986, p. 47.
2  Maeve Haran, *Having It All*, London: Signet, 1992, p. 4.
3  Diary of a new mother, http://news.bbc.co.uk/hi/english/health/newsid_751000/751205.stm
4  *Mother and Baby* magazine, published in the UK, November, 2001, pp. 16–17.
5  Ibid., p. 20.
6  Ibid., p. 18.
7  Maeve Haran, *Having it All*, London: Signet, 1992.
8  Ibid., p. 53.

9   A. Rich, *Of Woman Born*, New York: Bantam, 1976, quoted in
     A. Ferguson, 'On conceiving motherhood and sexuality: A
     materialist approach', in J. Treblicot (Ed.), *Mothering: Essays in
     Feminist Theory*, New Jersey: Rowman & Allanheld, p. 153.
10  Unattributed quote, *Mother and Baby* magazine, published in the
     UK, November, 2001, p. 6.
11  Germaine Greer, *The Whole Woman*, London: Anchor, 1999,
     p. 258.
12  Maeve Haran, *Having it All*, London: Signet, 1992, p. 2.
13  P. Nicolson, *Postnatal Depression: Facing the Paradox of Loss,
     Happiness and Motherhood*, Chichester: Wiley, 2001.
14  Ibid., p. 141.
15  Ibid., pp. 141–143.
16  Michael White, quoted on the BBC News web site
     http://news.bbc.co.uk/hi/english/business/newsid_1530000/
     1530355.stm
17  Susan Faludi, *Backlash: The Undeclared War against Women*,
     London: Vintage, 1992, p. 1.
18  Ibid., p. 107.
19  Quoted in HoustonChronicle.com 'Superwoman goes into retire-
     ment', October, 2001 wysiwyg://19/http://Houston. webpoint.
     com/job/yj67.htm

# Chapter 8

1   'Juggle don't struggle!' Paper produced for the British
     Government's Department of Trade and Industry (DTI) avail-
     able on the web site http://www.dti.gov.uk/work-lifebalance/
2   David Fontana, *Managing Stress*, Leicester: BPS Books, 1989,
     p. 1.
3   See Ricky Emanuel's book, *Anxiety*, Cambridge: Icon Books,
     2001. It is published in the Ideas in Psychoanalysis series, is
     short, to the point and readable.
4   Edward Charlesworth and Ronald Nathan, *Stress Management: A
     Comprehensive Guide to Wellness*, London: Souvenir Press, 1993,
     p. 203.

# Chapter 9

1   K. Browne, *Divided Labours: An Evolutionary View of Women at Work*, London: Weidenfeld & Nicolson, 1998.
2   Anne and Bill Moir, *Why Men Don't Iron: The New Reality of Gender Differences*, London: HarperCollins, 1999.
3   Danielle Crittenden, *What Our Mothers Didn't Tell Us: Why Happiness Eludes the Modern Woman*, New York: Simon & Schuster, 1999, quoted from the web site where the introduction is reproduced verbatim, p. 6, www.nytimes.com/books/first/c/crittended-mothers.html
4   Abridged in *The Times*, April 24, 2002, pp. 4–5, from the book by Sylvia Ann Hewlett: *Baby Hunger: The New Battle for Motherhood*, London: Atlantic Books, 2002.
5   Susie Orbach, *Towards Emotional Literacy*, London: Virago, 2001, p. 2.

# Index